#ProMa

Dinker Charak

Copyright © 2018 Dinker Charak

All rights reserved.

ISBN: 978-1-7322544-6-6

Imprint: Dinker Charak UNITED STATES

Contents

Early Praise for #ProMa v

Foreword..viii

Preface ix

Acknowledgment x

Introduction..xi

Product Management Tools & Methods

1. Hackathon: From an Idea to a Product in a Day 2
2. Product Backlog.. 14
3. Product Management Canvas.. 27
4. Competition Analysis in 3 Simple Steps 36
5. Taking In-House Product to Market 39
6. Go-To-Market Strategy in 4 Steps 50

Product Management Thoughts & Ideas

7. Can I Become a Good Product Manager?............................. 56
8. Product Thinking = ProMa + Design + Business Model 58
9. *Shuhari* & Software Evolution 61
10. Software Product: A Definition 64
11. Five Buckets Model for Product Management 65
12. The Product Sociologist 72
13. Are Non-Technical Product Managers Becoming Irrelevant? 74
14. Product Entrepreneurship v/s Product Management........ 75

15. Waterfall vs Agile: An Age-Old Battle 78

16. Product Development & The Scientific Process 80

17. It Takes a Village 87

18. 7 Reasons Why Your Product Will Fail 88

19. MVP of a Data Platform 91

Entrepreneurship

20. One Degree of Separation 94

21. The Most Memorable of Teams 97

22. Dirty-Work Group 98

23. Are Startups an MVP for Maslow's Hierarchy? 100

24. Our Children and The Digital Future 104

25. Startup Hiring Tips – The Golden Rule 107

26. Failing Since 2012 109

27. Lessons From a Failing Startup 138

About The Author 144

Appendix

List of Figures 148

List of Tables 151

Videos & Decks 152

Reference 154

Early Praise for #ProMa

"Who is my customer? Everybody, anyone you can think of—"

"Who is my competition? Amazon, Google, Netflix— (add any popular name in the Silicon Valley)."

"Who am I? I am a technology company who happens to do X (the industry this company should be in, till I probably walked in)."

This is what I keep hearing from the C-Suite at the clients I am engaged with.

In this world of needing and wanting to reinvent (or else — you are doomed), the most common response I have seen people resort to is to say that we have moved to a "product organization" or an "experience organization". This, no one will argue, needs change.

However, Dinker continues to argue that the challenges lie in the core philosophy. It's not an easy journey. I can guarantee you will fail if your thinking is that by reading this book, you will solve the challenges of "product thinking".

But here lies a great starting point from a great product philosopher, thinker, transformer, doer, practitioner, and above all, a great colleague and a friend.

Read on but engage with him when you get a chance. He will not fail to surprise you.

- Sagar Paul, Client Services - Strategic Accounts, at ThoughtWorks

Dinker is quirky, interdisciplinary, and full of real-world wisdom. The same could be said of this breezy new book on Product Management.

There are plenty of simple ProMa tools in our everyday use — 'Product in a Box' and 'Five buckets of Product Management' stand out. There is also the philosophical exploration of the subject through lenses as varied as Indian materialism, Francis Bacon (of the scientific method), and Rene Descartes. Most remarkably, there is a vivid tale of a failing startup — something any product entrepreneur will benefit from.

If you're a product manager or work with these sometimes-mysterious creatures, take a copy on your next flight. You'll have a spring in your step when you land.

- *Nagarjun Kandukuru, Principal Digital Strategist, ThoughtWorks*

A brilliant resource for all consultants — irrespective of the role they are in — and not just Product Managers. Dinker has poured his years of experience into this one book. He covers the entire lifecycle of a product/business evolution and introduces a lot of handy artifacts — checklists, frameworks, tools, etc. — that can be readily used at various stages of evolution. He sheds light on the real-life charms and challenges of building a product and does so in a simple yet eloquent manner. Keep an open mind and give this book a read — you'll thank him later for providing a wealth of knowledge on the topic.

- *Devangana Khokhar, Senior Data Scientist & Strategist, Thought-Works & Author Gephi Cookbook*

Dinker offers an enjoyable potpourri of helpful advice and ideas from his experience in consulting and his experiments with building products.

- Sriram Narayan, Digital-IT management consultant, Thought-Works & Author Agile IT Organization Design

Dinker is a magician — in a crisp book that is light and easy to read, he has packed in more than a semester's worth of high-priced B school education, and several years (and many dollars!) worth of lessons from a startup. Pick it up; you will not be disappointed.

- Naren Nachiappan, Co-Founder, Jivox

Foreword

Product Management remains one of the most misunderstood and misinterpreted roles in the software delivery today. In a world where technology is increasingly taking center stage, its fallen victim to being a handy bucket where all things ambiguous are dumped. However, in the current age of technology, it is taking center stage as one of the most critical roles in the software delivery lifecycle.

So, who is a Product Manager and what do they do? Having worked for a number of years on both sides of the fence — in Product firms as well as Service firms — I believe that it will be almost impossible to accurately define the role of a Product Manager: and realize that it probably ought to be this way. To be successful in this role, one needs a variety of different skills across the board, some inherent and some which can be acquired: curiosity, resilience, patience, agility, adaptability, amongst others.

So, if you get beyond the trivialities definitions and what defines Product Management and become interested in the specifics, this is for you. Dinker's collection of blogs are downright practical (with templates, tools, agendas, etc.) and serve as a step by step guide. I have had the good fortune and pleasure of being in workshops (the most memorable workshops have been the "Product in a Box" ones and his "It Takes a Village to build a Product" using WhatsApp — the most intriguing!) and talks Dinker has given and seen parts of this book grow over time.

As a parting warning, this book may appear to make the art of Product Management look easy. But like any art, it takes an effort to master it. To borrow a quote from the Matrix, "There is a difference between knowing the path and walking the path". Time to pop the Red Pill and get ready for the ride!

Sudhir Tiwari
(Managing Director ThoughtWorks India)
Feb 2018

Preface

This book is a direct result of my colleague, Sagar Paul, prodding me to collect my blog posts into a book so they can be shared as structured content.

This, along with encouragement I have received from other Thought-Workers (notably Sudhir Tiwari and Nagarjun Kandukuru) to keep blogging, has resulted in some ideas getting a life as written words.

I am especially thankful to Nagarjun Kandukuru, Steven McWhorter, Krishna Kumar Sure, and Nittish Veeraputhirasamy for their detailed feedback on the book.

The cover was done by Sunil Shrivastav and Advin Netto and is based on art by Sunil Shrivastav. Sunil and I have used this illustration often to describe a ProMa. They have both science and art, method and madness, grounded and dreamy, and tactical and strategic sides to them.

The term ProMa is short for Product Management. Along with being easy on the tongue, I think it reflects my slightly different look on ProMa. Different how? The chapters that follow will reveal that. You will encounter a collection of tools, methodologies, and unexpected approaches that promote lateral thinking.

Each chapter is complete in itself and focused on a specific theme. Some chapters may rely on concepts introduced in detail in a previous chapter. However, you can still benefit from it without knowing the details of the earlier chapters.

Some ideas are results of extended discussions, an opinion sought, or a point-of-view constructed for a client. All of them are the result of a sincere effort to produce something useful and usable — and at times, something unique.

Dinker Charak
18th Feb 2018

Acknowledgment

Special thanks to

Saneef Ansari, Soumitra Bajpai, Avik Chatterjee, Suganth Chellamuthu, Arjun Dev, Navneet Gosal, Munish Jauhar, Shaun Jayaraj, Nagarjun Kandukuru, Jiangmei Kang, Kartik Kannan, Priyanka Kapur, Sanjay Kumar, Smita Kumari, Sharon Lackey, Wairok Makunga, Kiran Manapragada, Steven McWhorter, Naren Nachiappan, Sriram Narayan, Diaz Nesamoney, Advin Netto, Anantpal Singh Saluja, Sagar Paul, Sachin Sapre, Sharath Satish, Sunil Shrivastav, Krishna Kumar Sure, Sudhir Tiwari, Piyush Trivedi, Mudit Varma, Prasanna J Vaste, Margaret Votava.

Introduction

This is the second edition of the book. It came about when I decided to publish a paper version to follow the fast-growing Kindle version.

#ProMa is a collection of blog posts that I have written over the past few years.

This book is useful to anyone who wishes to be or is already a Product Manager. Founders tend to be the first Product Managers. In that light, it is good for Startup Founders too. Experienced Product Managers will encounter some ideas that may help them redefine their roles and use lateral thinking to reinvent their approach to the day-to-day tasks.

This book is divided into three sections.

The first section (chapters 1-6) is on various tools & methods that I have created and used for Product Management. These include the Product Management Canvas and the Product workshops I run.

The second section (chapters 7-19) is on various thoughts and ideas that I have around what it means to be a Product Managers and around Product Management itself.

The third section (chapters 20-27) is on entrepreneurship and it is based on my experience as a founder who hasn't succeeded yet. It also has some ideas on team building that revolves around a novel concept called 'Dirty-Work Group'.

I have added a new chapter in this edition on how to design the MVP of a Platform.

Dinker Charak
22nd Apr, 2018

Product Management Tools & Methods

1.
HACKATHON: FROM AN IDEA TO A PRODUCT IN A DAY

I have conducted one-day Product Management workshops for CIIE, IIM Ahmedabad's Entrepreneur Cell[1], NASSCOM 10,000 Startups[2,3] and various offices of ThoughtWorks.

We start with a new idea or an existing idea, work through it over the day, focus on one key product to come up with a clear picture of what it will be and an MVP for it. The audience has been the whole spectrum: folks who came in with an idea, startups that came with a prototype, or startups that are just beginning to some customer traction.

Over time, a structure has emerged and that is what I will be sharing here — it is going to be a long one.

My comments will work under the assumption that the participants are startups that have spent some time on the idea and have a prototype in the market. However, this approach will also work for the whole spectrum I mentioned above.

Here is what a typical agenda looks like:

Agenda

9:00 AM	Our Approach, Objectives and Ground Rules	0:30
9:30 AM	Product in a Box	0:30
10:00 AM	Elevator Pitch	0:30

10:30 AM	Business Model Canvas *Value Prop., Customer Segments & Channels*	1:00
11:30 AM	*Break*	*0:15*
11:45 AM	Business Model Canvas *Cost & Revenues*	1:00
12:45 PM	*Lunch Break*	*0:45*
1:30 PM	Product Strategy *Products line-up & Prioritization*	0:30
2:00 PM	Product Management Canvas *Idea, Market, Customer Segment, Business Value & Metrics*	1:00
3:00 PM	*Break*	*0:15*
3:15 PM	Product Management Canvas *Features, Evangelism, Go-To-Market, Visual Identity & Key Resources*	1:00
4:15 PM	*Break*	*0:30*
4:45 PM	Identifying MVP *Using Product Management Canvas to identify an MVP*	0:45
5:30 PM	Done	

Table 1-1: Hackathon Agenda

The day is run on a very tight schedule. So, it is important to stick to time. Also, the aim is breadth-first and cover all rather than depth-first and iron out details.

This allows the attendees to get familiar with the methods so they can do a detailed version on their own.

The Approach, Objectives and Ground Rules

This is similar to any Inception[4]. One thing I always bring out is that I will openly discuss each team's idea with all the participants. Folks attending should be comfortable sharing their ideas with the group.

I always allow mobile phones. Folks are going to be here all day, typically on a Saturday. A few minutes of phone calls related to family and work is not very disruptive as long as they step out before taking the call.

Product in a Box

Sometimes referred to as Product Box[5], it is a Product in a Box. Luke Hohmann. Accessed January 2018. Innovation Games: Creating Breakthrough Products Through Collaborative Play 1st Edition fun activity in which everyone is asked to imagine if their product came in a box, what the label of the box would look like. I provide this empty sheet to participants:

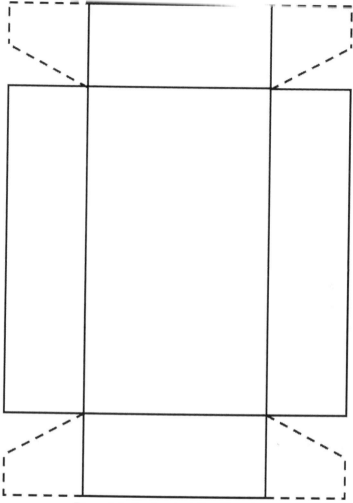

Figure 1-1: Product in A Box Template

In order to help them visualize and organize their thoughts, I show them this slide for reference and walk them through each section and give some examples.

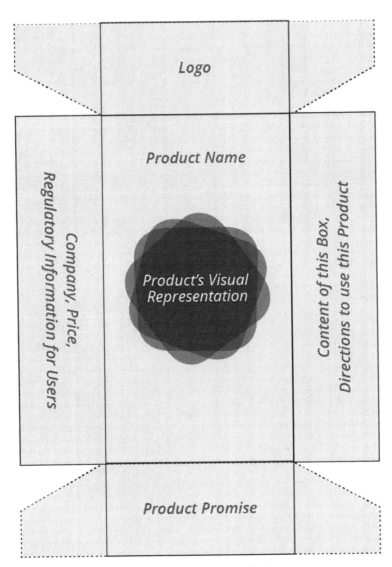

Figure 1-2: Product in A Box Reference

Usually, people struggle a bit with this. It's either they are lost for words or they begin to write too much text and end up frozen! Also, this being the first session, folks are a bit slow to get started. What I usually suggest is that they just start writing. Once they do, words follow words and they are able to finish.

Once they are all done (15 mins), I request each to read out exactly what they have written and add nothing as an afterthought. I then ask all if they will be willing to buy/invest in the idea.

The very exercise of having to write out the thoughts, read them aloud, not add in an ad-hoc manner to it, and then hear responses, sets the time for the rest of the day. I stress a lot about brevity and simplicity.

Elevator Pitch

We have a very good format for an Elevator Pitch[6] that I often use. We give them a printed page which has an outline of an Elevator Pitch that they have to complete. Having gone through the Product in a Box exercise earlier and heard the feedback, folks just go swiftly through this and are able to come up with excellent articulations. The format looks like this:

Figure 1-3: Elevator Pitch Template

Note: I have reversed the order and done Elevator Pitch first before Product in a Box. But in either case, attendees struggle with the first one and then do the next one rather fast and nicely.

Business Model Canvas

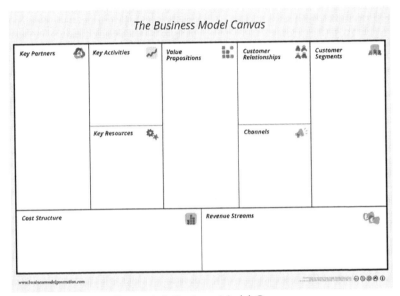

Figure 1-4: Business Model Canvas

We do Business Model Canvas[7] in two sessions.

Session 1

I first ask them to write down the key Value Props. This is followed by writing down the various Customer Segments. The key is to narrow them down as much as possible. So, using words like 'All' are discouraged.

Then I ask them to make a line for each Value Prop to each Customer Segment it serves. Ideally, all Value Props should serve some segment and all segments should have some value prop for them. If none, the customer segment needs to go.

Then I ask them to name a channel for each Value Prop. At least one channel for each stage of Brand Awareness Funnel. That is, Awareness, Consideration, Engagement, and then Purchase.

In my previous life, my work on Brand Awareness Funnel was converted into a patent[8] by my organization at the time.

Session 2

In this session, we focus on Cost and Revenue. Surprisingly, helping startups that have been around realize their cost is the most a-ha/oh-sh*t moment. Perpetual optimists like Founders rarely internalize the cost of getting things done and this serves as a good eye-opener. A lot of time is spent on the revenue side of things.

I usually help them with quick back-of-envelope calculations. Salaries of founders, office rent, internet bills, laptops, furniture, folks for sales, support, development, CA, filings, buying compute power, licenses, fees, etc., and soon the estimates balloon.

The session on revenue is a lot shorter. I ask them to write down all the possible avenues of revenues and then estimate revenues it can bring in over time along with the complexity of making that revenue. This helps them prioritize one avenue over another.

Product Strategy

This session was added after the initial few workshops. When asked questions like: What are the products your company builds? What is your key product? What components does your product have? What products are you working on to enable your key product? I used to get very vague answers. Most of them would start talking about their awesome app.

The thing is that without realizing how much effort the company is putting into various products (in-house, customer facing, partner facing, admin tools, 3rd-party integrations, stuff that 3rd Parties can use, etc.), it was often apparent that they were not looking at the whole picture of the whole product when prioritizing.

So, I came with this Product Stack[9] template:

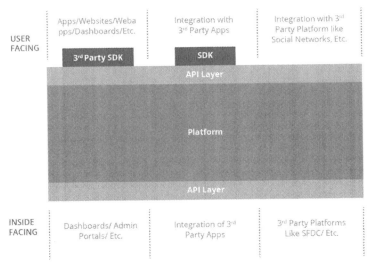

Figure 1-5: Product Stack Template

I ask them to fill this up with all things they are using and have built. The output surprises everyone. Once they have listed them all, I ask them to mark out the ones the company cannot proceed as a business without. This eliminates a lot of random legacy products they have accumulated over time and focus on the ones that really matter.

Two things can also happen while performing this exercise:

1. We force them to think beyond Channels (like apps, websites, etc.) and think in terms of the whole Platform.

2. Get them into the exercise of prioritizing engineering output and not jump into creating apps, websites, etc., without creating a roadmap at a strategic level.

Note: In case of new ideas, I ask them to list down things they will need to use and build. They then prioritize based on that.

Product Management Canvas

Once the key product has been reinforced, identified or agreed upon, we use the Product Management Canvas[10] to describe it.

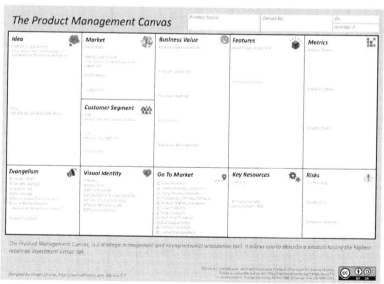

Figure 1-6: Product Management Canvas

Lots of content flows in from the canvases and work done in the previous sessions. That makes filling up this canvas faster. The only thing is that these are not at the level of the entire business but at the level of this product. This means the slice of whole business canvas that this product addresses.

We recommend that they do it for each of their key products. Product Managers can use it for their products. I talk more about Product Management Canvas in chapter 3.

Identifying MVP

One thing that the Product Management Canvas helps with is in identifying an MVP. Here is how I put it:

"Specific Features that deliver extreme value to a specific Customer Segment and helps attain specific Business Value using specific Key Resources measured using related Success and Failure Metrics with right Visual Identity and Go-To-Market support."

The Product Management Canvas helps identify the MVP that should be rolled out first.

Preparation for the Workshop

To prepare, I print out some canvases. Here are the list and size of paper on which they are printed.

Product in A Box	A4
Elevator Pitch	A4
Business Model Canvas	A3
Product Management Canvas	A3

Table 1-2: Suggested Paper Size for Various Artifacts

Using A3 gives some real estate to write down on the Business Model Canvas and the Product Model Canvas.

A version of this appeared on www.ddiinnxx.com. A related article appeared on ThoughtWorks Insight https://thght.works/2G4BQ0O. A slide deck version of it is available on SlideShare: http://bit.ly/2nWx8LQ. A PDF version of it is available on http://bit.ly/2qncrvO.

2.
Product Backlog

I propose a method to build a Product Backlog, how to record a feature that has a clearly quantified business value, and how this fits into a specific project's inception.

Backlog Definition from Agile Alliance[1]

> A backlog is a list of features or technical tasks which the team maintains and which, at a given moment, are known to be necessary and sufficient to complete a project or a release:
>
> - if an item on the backlog does not contribute to the project's goal, it should be removed;
>
> - on the other hand, if at any time a task or feature becomes known that is considered necessary to the project, it should be added to the backlog.

These "necessary and sufficient" properties are assessed relative to the team's state of knowledge at a particular moment; the backlog is expected to change throughout the project's duration as the team gains knowledge.

The backlog is the primary point of entry for knowledge about requirements, and the single authoritative source defining the work to be done.

Not That Backlog

Various terms exist for a backlog being used in Agile development. Based on scope, tradition, terms such as Story Backlog, Feature Backlog, Epics Backlog, Development Backlog, and at times, Product Backlog too is used.

I will refer to these as Story Backlog so I can differentiate it with the Product backlog I am introducing in this write-up.

Story Backlog Definition from Mountain Goat Software[2]

> The agile story backlog in Scrum is a prioritized features list, containing short descriptions of all functionality desired in the product. A typical Scrum backlog comprises the following different types of items:
>
> - Features
> - Bugs
> - Technical work
> - Knowledge acquisition

Story Backlog Definition from Atlassian[3]

> A story backlog is a prioritized list of work for the development team that is derived from the roadmap and its requirements. The most important items are shown at the top of the story backlog so the team knows what to deliver first. The development team doesn't work through the backlog at the product owner's pace and the product owner isn't pushing work to the development team. Instead, the development team pulls work from the story backlog as there is capacity for it, either continually (kanban) or by iteration (scrum).

Product Backlog

A Product Backlog is a prioritized features list, containing short descriptions of all functionality desired in the product, with a business value for each feature clearly quantified along with the source of the feature request or inspiration.

Product Backlog Card

A look at what a Product Backlog Card can look like:

ID	
Theme / Module	
Action – Expected Result / I want to – So That / Feature / Inception time Epic	
Assumptions	
Priority	
Value Ranking	
Success Metric (to judge value delivered)	
Failure Metric (to trigger a re-learn/re-analyze)	
Status	
Source	

Table 2-1: Product Backlog Card Template

I am still not sure if Priority would still make sense given that Value Ranking is there. The reason I have added it is because Priority represents the perspective of the person who is creating this card and Value Ranking is a quantitative analysis based on weightage. Value Ranking is a kind of check on the 'gut feel' or 'emotional' Priority.

I think Source is important. We should link back to the CRM entry, the social media post, a market study, email, etc., that lead to the creation of this. It is important to refer to that original content which can be referred to as-is in the future and considered as an 'interpretation-free' source which a ProMa used.

Scoping Product Backlog Card

How much work is a feature? There are some questions that a ProMa should ask to give Business Analysts, Iteration Managers and Developers a good idea of the breadth of work involved. There is, always, more to a feature than just implementation. Look at the suggested list to get an idea of what I mean here:

Time	Is a Go-To-Market time identified?
	If yes, date?
Collateral	Does it need marketing collaterals?
	Does it need sales collaterals?
	Does it need support collaterals?
	Does it need user collaterals?
Change Management	Does it need a change in process?

	Does it need a change in people & behavior?
	Does it need a change in how users interact?
	Does it need a change in tech?
Control	Does it bring in regulatory & legal aspect?
	Does it bring in un-handled regulatory & legal aspect?
	Does it need extra/new licenses?
	Does it get covered by existing license model?
Measurement	Are the proper measurement mechanisms in place?
Security & Safety	Does it need extra security focus?

Table 2-2: Template for Scoping Feature

A 'yes' on any of these will affect the scope of work not only for the developers but for others too. It is important to look beyond the functionality during implementation.

Quantifying Product Vision using Rubrics

A feature can be seen to provide/contribute to one or more of the following values at various levels:

- BAU
- Strategic
- Competitive
- Collaborative
- Revenue
- Cost

Based on the vision, these six can be given various weightage.

E.g.: 1/ A product like say 'Am-Behind App' is playing catch up on feature parity with its competition. The weightage can be:

BAU	10%
Strategic	10%
Competitive	40%
Collaborative	10%
Revenue	20%
Cost	10%

E.g.: 2/ A product like say 'Am-Expensive App' is focused on reducing capex. The weightage can be:

BAU	10%
Strategic	10%
Competitive	5%
Collaborative	5%
Revenue	20%

Cost	50%

E.g.: 3/ A product like say 'Want-2-Breakfree App' is focused on growth through usual and innovative methods. The weightage can be:

BAU	25%
Strategic	30%
Competitive	40%
Collaborative	0%
Revenue	5%
Cost	0%

And so on. This should give a quantitative representation of your product's vision. This should not change too often. Changes to it will change the 'value rank' of a feature as we will see below.

However, it is expected to change given the Build-Measure-Learn nature of ProMa. The change will drive a new priority against which the Product Backlog can be re-prioritized.

Quantifying Value

Start with asking some key questions around these vision directions. These are illustrative and a ProMa can formulate their own based on their context. This questionnaire needs to be designed carefully and in collaboration with key stakeholders to ensure that the right criteria are added and weighed.

BAU	Does it address a key market?
	Does it add to the USP/Key Value Prop?
Strategic	Does it open up new market opportunities?
	Does it offer a significant competitive advantage?
	Are early adopters identified?
Competitive	Does it allow us to catch up with specific competition (e.g., feature parity)?
	Does it allow a 'we-too-have-it' comparison against specific competition?
Collaborative	Does it contribute to or benefit from a 'free' software ecosystem?
	Does it contribute to or benefit from a "paid" software ecosystem?
Cost	Does it bring cost benefit?
Revenue	Does it enable potential revenue uplift?
	Does it lead to revenue uplift indirectly?
	Does it lead to revenue uplift directly?

Table 2-3: Template for Scoping Feature

The answers can be Yes or No and quantified as 1 or 0. A Yes will lead to a value of 1 * weightage. We can add up all the values and arrive at a value rank.

E.g., For the product 'Want-2-Breakfree App', a feature has been requested that allows it to address a similar need but in a different domain. With this vision weightage:

BAU   25%

Strategic   30%

Competitive   40%

Collaborative   0%

Revenue   5%

Cost   0%

This is how feature analysis and value rank can look like:

BAU	Does it address a key market?	Yes	25
	Does it add to the USP/Key Value Prop?	Yes	25
Strategic	Does it open up new market opportunities?	No	0
	Does it offer a significant competitive advantage?	Yes	30
	Are early adopters identified?	Yes	30
Competitive	Does it allow us to catch up with specific competition (e.g., feature parity)?	Yes	40

	Does it allow a 'we-too-have-it' comparison against specific competition?	No	0
Collaborative	Does it contribute to or benefit from a "free" software ecosystem?	No	0
	Does it contribute to or benefit from a "paid" software ecosystem?	No	0
Cost	Does it bring cost benefit?	Yes	5
Revenue	Does it enable potential revenue uplift?	No	0
	Does it lead to revenue uplift indirectly?	Yes	0
	Does it lead to revenue uplift directly?	No	0
			155

Table 2-4: Example for Scoping Feature A

Now let us see for another feature. A feature has been requested that allows it to analyze the response via various marketing channels. This is how feature analysis and value rank can look like:

BAU	Does it address a key market?	Yes	25
	Does it add to the USP/ Key Value Prop?	Yes	25

Strategic	Does it open up new market opportunities?	Yes	30
	Does it offer a significant competitive advantage?	Yes	30
	Are early adopters identified?	Yes	30
Competitive	Does it allow us to catch up with specific competition (e.g., feature parity)?	Yes	40
	Does it allow a 'we-too-have-it' comparison against specific competition?	No	0
Collaborative	Does it contribute to or benefit from a "free" software ecosystem?	No	0
	Does it contribute to or benefit from a "paid" software ecosystem?	No	0
Cost	Does it bring cost benefit?	Yes	5
Revenue	Does it enable potential revenue uplift?	Yes	0
	Does it lead to revenue uplift indirectly?	Yes	0
	Does it lead to revenue uplift directly?	No	0
			185

Table 2-5: Example for Scoping Feature B

So, the later feature (B) should be prioritized higher in the Product Backlog.

Product Backlog and Inceptions

How does a Product Backlog fit into the larger Product Inception[4]? It is important to call out here that a Product development may be done via multiple projects. Thus, a Product Inception can lead to multiple Project Inceptions.

Questions have been asked on how to introduce the Product Thinking and Product Management roles during a Project Inception.

As of today, this is how I see the flow:

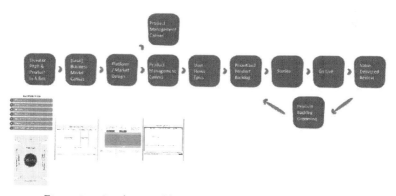

Figure 2-1: Product Backlog in Product Development Process

This flow is heavily influenced by experience on one day Product Management workshop that has been attended by over 100 folks till now and various inceptions I have attended.

We follow the same visioning as we do in Inception. However, when we do epics, we convert them into a Product Backlog. Each Product Backlog will lead to multiple stories. What is different in a Product

Backlog is some quantification of business value that it delivers and metrics on how to measure it.

When stories go live and get consumed by users, we can measure and learn. This learning is brought back as part of analysis and grooming on the Product backlog (not Story or Development Backlog).

Re-prioritization of Product Backlog can affect the stories that get picked up next.

A version of this appeared on www.ddiinnxx.com.

3.
PRODUCT MANAGEMENT CANVAS

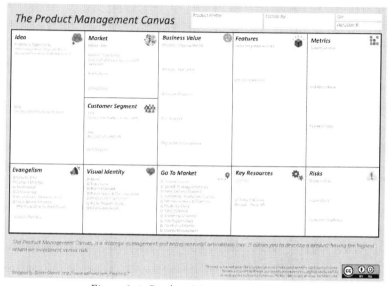

Figure 3-1: Product Management Canvas

The Product Management Canvas (PMC) is a strategic management and entrepreneurial articulation tool. It allows one to describe a product having the highest return on investment versus risk.

I envision its purpose as different from that of a Product Model Canvas or Roman Pichler's Product Canvas[1].

This Product Management Canvas captures the product in one canvas and gives a good 360-degree view. It represents a sufficient definition of the product that can easily be shared within your organization.

Where Does Product Management Canvas Fit?

Let us understand the Product Flow. I talked about it in detail in the Hackathon: From Idea to a Product in a Day chapter.

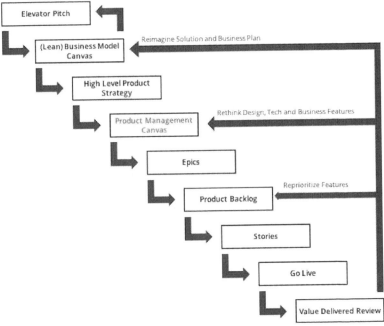

Figure 3-2: Product Management Canvas in Product Development Process

To summarize the flow diagram:

Using Elevator Pitch & Product in a Box, we describe the product we want to build. However, no product exists in a vacuum and is part of an ecosystem. We then layout the Product Ecosystem that enables the key product. The product is then described using the Product Management Canvas.

A Product Management Canvas then informs the process of Epics (a large body of work that describes a coherent capability that can be broken into multiple stories[2]). Adding a business case to these, we arrive at a Product Backlog that I discussed in detail in chapter 2. Each item in the Product Backlog can lead to one or more stories[3]. When these stories Go Live and the products hit the market, in the spirit of build-measure-learn, we learn and periodically do the Product Backlog Grooming.

The Elevator Pitch & Product In A Box, Business Model Canvas or Lean Business Model Canvas, High-Level Products Layout, and Product Management Canvas are explained in the blog post above.

Epics, Product Backlog, Stories and Build-Measure-Learn are standard terms that are described as part of the Agile process.

I believe that this sits one step before Roman Pichler's Product Canvas and is used to plan and describe a product instead of tracking the agile product creation/development.

Understanding the Product Management Canvas

The canvas started as a checklist for Product Managers to ensure they have not missed any aspect of Product planning. However, it was always aimed at capturing the current state of an evolving product. Thus, Product Management Canvas should be used to communicate across various groups and departments to ensure that all have the same picture of the product.

Using the Product Management Canvas

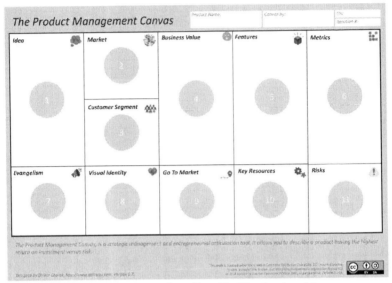

Figure 3-3: Suggested Flow for Filling Up The Product Management Canvas

The suggested flow is:

1. Idea
2. Market
3. Customer Segment
4. Business Value
5. Features
6. Metrics
7. Evangelism
8. Visual Identity
9. Go-To-Market
10. Key Resources
11. Risks

Now, let us look at each section in detail:

Idea

We start with describing the original **problem or opportunity** that the product addresses. It can be a unique need, a dormant need (we are creating the market), or an aspiration (of the user/customer) that needs to be addressed.

Once the above is stated, it is important to connect it with what the **idea** of the product and state how it addresses the above.

Market

Start by stating the **market size** (defined as the market volume or the market potential). VCs will want this to be a very big number — big enough to accommodate you and all your competition.

Then state the **market opportunity** your product addresses from the whole market size. This should be a more realistic number that should allow sufficient growth so you can give investors a good rate of return.

A product never exists in a vacuum. There is an ecosystem of **partners** that enable it. We should note all key partners (data suppliers, data consumers, channels, SDKs, and so on).

What's fun without any **competition?** It is important to note the competition and track them. If you have analyzed the competition in detail, you can add the link to that document. My thoughts on how to do Competition Analysis is found in chapter 4.

Customer Segment

Identifying if the product is **B2B** or **B2C** is sometimes obvious. But going one level deeper is important.

Does my B2B target Startup, SME, Business Houses, MNC, etc.? Or does my B2C target BPL (Below Poverty Line), LMC (Lower Middle Class), MC (Middle Class), UMC (Upper Middle Class), HNI (High Networth Individuals), etc.?

Also important is identifying **Early Adopters**, Influencers, Recommenders and Innovators who try something new.

Business Value

Large organizations that create a lot of products need to ensure that there is a **product-organization fit**. This would involve making sure that the product fits into an established ecosystem, reuses tools, etc., and does not create whole parallel infrastructure requirements.

The **product–market fit** is very important and needs to be articulated crisply.

There are many **revenue models** available and many times the same product will have multiples of them. State the considered revenue models in this section.

Cost Analysis is a complex task but having a broad idea of the cost of producing the product that reflects the pricing model is recorded. Even when the aim is to invest in seeding the product, it is important to state and communicate the revenue–cost ratio.

It is important to state the key **Regulatory & Compliance** items. These should not slip through the cracks of day-to-day tasks.

Features

It is important to state the **Value Propositions/USP** (Unique Selling Proposition) and communicate it uniformly. Not every differentiation is a USP, nor should it be. Along with USP, the other **key features** that set us apart, make usage simple or make us better than our competition should also be noted.

Metrics

We all talk about **success metrics**. But before a product is successful, there are some minimal metrics a product should achieve. These should not be 'not meeting success metrics,' but independent ones.

E.g., while achieving an MAU (Monthly Active Users[4]) of 1M is the success for your chat app, the number of messages exchanged if not growing at the same rate as user adoption is a **failure metric**.

Failure metrics are important as they tell us how key hypotheses could be wrong, alerting us that it is time to reassess them and relearn and rebuild.

Viability metrics are good to have to make sure we are on track to success or being a financially viable product.

Evangelism

Product evangelism is, as Guy Kawasaki put it years ago, "selling the dream". It's helping people to imagine the future and inspiring them to help create that future[5].

Many things need to fall into place for an Evangelist to be effective. This section offers a checklist of essential items needed to enable an evangelist.

This includes an **elevator pitch**, a story to tell, relevant content generation is a **content strategy** to keep it updated, uniform **terminology** across all departments and collaterals, **SEO strategy** so content is geared to show up in right searches, right **brand assets**, and **social media presence**.

Using all possible social networks is not the right approach. Choose and state the ones that are relevant to the product, the audience and manageable by the team.

Visual Identity

This section offers a checklist of essential items needed to establish a **visual identity**.

Product name, logo, icons, brand playbook, presentation/docs/stationery templates, product docs templates, social network assets (cover picture, etc.), and display ad assets.

Go-To-Market

This section offers a checklist of essential items to formulate an effective go-to-market strategy.

In the case of a new product, **time of launch** is an important date/period. A product Manager should initiate and collaborate in the **launch strategy** & related **collaterals**, describing **sales** and product **delivery channels**, **positioning** & **promotion strategy**, identify and help reach out to **decision-makers**, **influencers** & **recommenders**, **sales collateral**, **marketing collateral**, **user support docs**, and **training collaterals**.

Often, a product leads to changes in processes and roles of people. The product manager has to think about a **change management** template.

Key Resources

Stating key resources is important as it allows a product manager to track them. This includes various tools, **licenses** (e.g., SSL licenses as anybody can forget to renew on time like Google[6], Instagram[7], and Apple[8]), **3rd party platforms** like **SDK, analytics tools**, etc.

Risks

State the known **shortcomings** and **assumptions** made. This helps plan the build-measure-learn better.

Product managers need to be paranoid about the product getting disrupted. It is important to consider **Disruption Readiness** by identifying processes and methods that can be replaced all at once.

A version of this appeared on www.ddiinnxx.com.

4.
COMPETITION ANALYSIS IN 3 SIMPLE STEPS

Want to get with Competition Analysis in 3 Simple Steps? Yes, only 3!

Step 1: Being Competitive Means?

What does it mean to be competitive? What is the purpose of competition? And finally, what does it mean to compete? Every business needs to be clear on these questions.

I have used this very often to get all focus on the right competition and the expected outcome of being competitive. This is a simple visualization by Flow Ventures[1]:

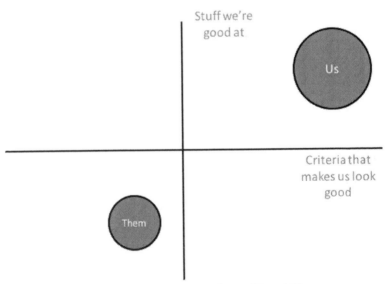

Figure 4-1: Competition Analysis – Us and Them

Step 2: Listing Competition

Competitive landscape is a spectrum. Not all competition is a threat. We need to list our potentials across the whole spectrum. I have used the following 4 headings to help clients list out competition.

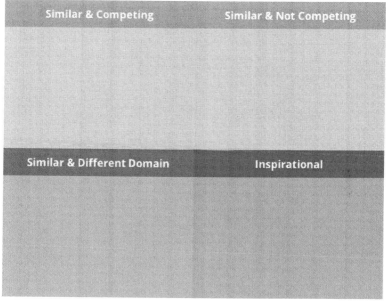

Figure 4-2: The Four Boxes of Competition Analysis

Step 3. Competition Deep Dive

Identify key competition(s) from each block and do a deep dive. Here is one canvas to help structure it:

#ProMa

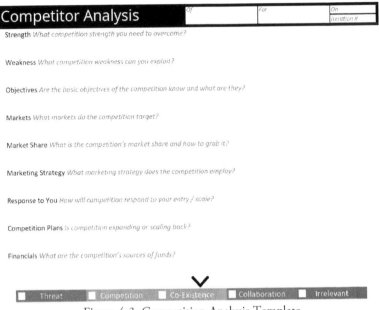

Figure 4-3: Competition Analysis Template

Conclusion

To revisit some thoughts:

- Be clear on why your business needs to be competitive and the expected outcome
- Competitive landscape is a spectrum
- Not all competition is a threat (at a given point)
- Identify competitions from each block on the spectrum and do a deep dive

A version of this appeared on www.ddiinnxx.com.

5.
TAKING IN-HOUSE PRODUCT TO MARKET

Exploring how to take a product that was built for internal use by a company to market. Starting with why it could/should be done, discussing the stages in which this can be done, specific tasks for a Product Manager, and finally, the various tasks for various teams. Almost a great checklist to keep around.

1. Intro

1.1 Internal vs External

Folks at Proficientz[1] differentiated the two by using three important dimensions:

	Internal	External
Terminology	Project Portfolio	Product Portfolio
Impact	Cost	Revenue
Focus	Efficiency	Market

Table 5-1: Internal vs External

2. The Why

2.1 Why Take to Market

- Revenue Potential
- Employee Morale

- Leadership
    - Thought
    - Technology
    - Product
    - Design
    - Domain
    - Engineering
    - Practices

2.2 Five Questions to Start With

- Who ELSE will buy this?

Names of likely buyers and categories of buyers. The reason 'else' is emphasized is to highlight that there is already one customer — your own org.

- What options will they reject to buy this?

Similar products or option to custom-build.

- For what key benefit do you think they will pay?

The USP/Key Value Prop.

- How much and how do you think they will pay for this?

First take on Pricing and pricing model.

- Why would your org support this effort?

A powerful reason.

3. The How

3.1 The Golden Logarithmic Spiral

First thing to keep in mind:

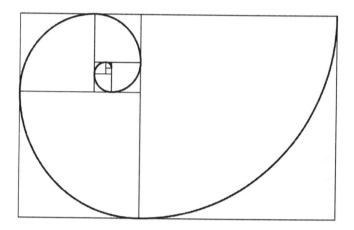

Figure 5-1: Golden Logarithmic Spiral

The complexity in each stage of this process will increase logarithmically. Remember this spiral very well.

3.2 Six Stages of Business Rollout

An External Product will be exponentially more complex when compared to its in-house version.

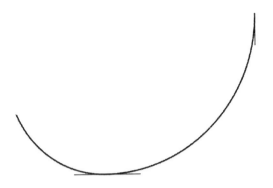

Figure 5-2: Internal to External - The Golden Curve

The left side of this cup implies that as we climb down from what has been built/learned till now, and unlearn, the complexity will decrease.

However, as we re-analyze and then start the process, the complexity will grow exponentially.

The stages:

3.2.1 Unlearn

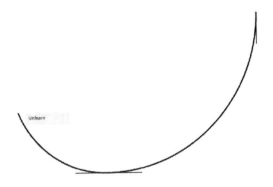

Figure 5-3: Internal to External - Stage 1

Unlearning is very important. In any future crisis, resorting to what worked earlier can be disastrous. Doing experiments anew is important.

3.2.2 Re-Analyze

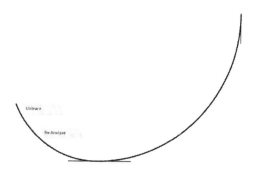

Figure 5-4: Internal to External - Stage 2

Starting with 5 Questions mentioned earlier, it is important to re-analyze the product, its reason and benefits with a whole market in view.

3.2.3 Early Access

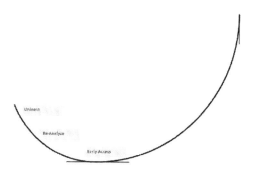

Figure 5-5: Internal to External - Stage 3

A good time to test many hypotheses.

3.2.4 Limited Access

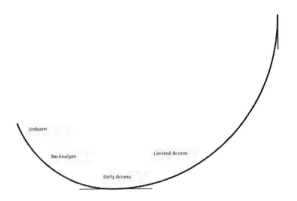

Figure 5-6: Internal to External - Stage 4

There is less Complexity when compared to your present state.

3.2.5 Open Access

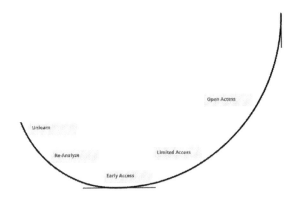

Figure 5-7: Internal to External - Stage 5

There is a lot more Complexity than you could ever face in-house. Although you should plan for it, there is no point guessing/estimating this and beyond. Thus, take the lean approach.

3.2.6 Self-Serve

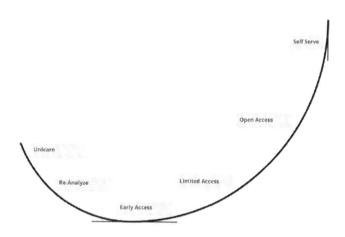

Figure 5-8: Internal to External - Stage 6

Although you should plan for it, there is no point guessing/estimating this and beyond. Thus, continue to take lean approach.

3.2.7 In Detail

Figure 5-9: Internal to External – Tasks at Various Stages

3.3 Seven Tasks for the ProMa

- Get a Design team to work on branding assets and reassessing the user flow and experience

- Get a Product team to redo the Product Management Canvas

- Get a Quality team to check that the product will work well when it is opened up

- Get a Security team to analyze the risks associated with opening the product

- Get a Marketing team to brand and deliver collaterals, articles, blogs, ads, etc.

- Get a Support team that is ready to help users as if their lives depended on it
- Get a Sales team that will go and search for booking & revenues

3.4 Twenty-Five Actions for the Teams

3.4.1 Design

1. Design an independent branding and design language
2. Rethink user flows and user experiences based on user research as 100% of new users may not be directly accessible

3.4.2 Product

3. Rethink your MVP
4. Redefine the product vision
5. Take control of Roadmap and break free of the shackles of Product Sponsor and early advocates
6. Remove confidential analysis, techniques and flows
7. Re-assess the product-market fit
8. Take your competition more seriously and not just as a source for ideas
9. Revisit rejected partners and rebuild an ecosystem
10. Add Role Management to accommodate Admins and Super-Admins
11. Re-access tech decisions on tools, stacks, and methods
12. Start saying NO to requests from Product Sponsors or early users
13. Consider licensing
14. Consider the threat of piracy and security breaches

3.4.3 Feedback, Support, Marketing & Communication

15. Build searchable and easily navigable knowledge base to enable self-discovery
16. Add an option to report bugs, provide feedback, and request support from within the product
17. Add an option to report bugs, provide feedback, and request support using social media
18. Incentivize or reward communication from users and partners
19. Reach out and market using social media and do not hesitate to advertise

3.4.4 Business & Commercial

20. Add 'buying' of product, even if it is for $0
21. Establish a pricing/discounting/packaging policy
22. Retrain your teams to focus on revenues and set up an efficient revenue tracking system
23. Make 'buying' or e-commerce via your product simple

3.4.5 Organization

24. Get a dedicated team
25. Get branding, support, marketing, and sales teams in place

4. Best Practices

4.1 For Open Sourcing

- Technical Communication
- Version Control, Document Management, and Distribution
- Quality Assurance
- Build and Test Management
- Project Management

- Knowledge Management

4.2 For Commercializing

- Clear pricing policy
- Easy to understand licensing policy
- Easy to report bugs and provide feedback
- Continuous security analysis and piracy protection
- Easy to use e-commerce and buy option
- Ability to define roles and grant permissions
- Self-discovery via knowledge management
- Support (free and paid variants)
- Enables 3rd parties to build products or provide service on top of your product
- Analytics

A version of this appeared on www.ddiinnxx.com. A slide deck version of it is available on SlideShare: http://bit.ly/2nXZrsu.

6.
GO-TO-MARKET STRATEGY IN 4 STEPS

To develop a Go-To-Market (GTM) Strategy, I suggest following four steps:

Step 1: Know Your Product Well

There is an awesome Dilbert comic where he is introduced to "Kenny The Sales Weasel". Both of them are to work on a big prospect and Dilbert is expected to explain to him about the product.

The comic is about how knowing products is of no importance in the weasel-world!

It is OK for Sales superstars in Dilbert's world to know little about the product. But you have to know it very well to devise a successful Go-to-market strategy. Not only that, you should also be able to describe it in sufficient detail to other departments in your company.

Product Management Canvas is one such tool. It captures the product in one canvas and gives a good 360-degree view.

Step 2: Ask Yourself Three Fundamental Questions

What to sell?

What exactly are you selling? This has to be articulated for each customer segment and each value prop.

Many times, a solution could come from the combinations of your products. In this case, the above needs to be done for all product combinations.

Whom to sell to?

Depending on if you are a new product or a mature product, your userbase and customers would differ.

If you are a new product, identify key influencers, usual suspects among early adopters, and focus on reaching an early majority.

If you are a matured product, identify key late majority and laggards. Decision makers in large enterprises (like the CTO's office or the Procurement division) can help you situate yourself stronger while the product team keeps innovating to keep your product relevant to your client.

The key is to identify the right recommenders and decision influencers for long-term success.

How to sell?

Pricing is complex. Sometimes, it is easy to start with tiered prices that allow you to serve small-scale, small-budget customers to generate revenue while hunting for large ones. You must have seen some like this:

Figure 6-1: Sample Pricing Table

Your Pricing strategy should have such Pricing models and option to use channels to accelerate sales.

Step 3: Understand the Sales Funnel

We know the typical sales funnel. It is the journey of your customer from when they become aware of your product to when they actually buy it and when they choose to rebuy it.

The journey in short:

Awareness -> Consideration -> Research -> Selection -> Purchase -> Delivery -> Support -> Repeat Purchase -> Recommendation to Buy

Understanding this is very important and you should plan on how to egg your customers on to the next stage.

Step 4: Work on These Nineteen Tasks

1. Time of Launch
2. Launch Strategy and Collaterals
3. Sales and Delivery Channels
4. Positioning and Promotion Strategy
5. Decision Makers and Influencers
6. Recommenders
7. Sales Collateral
8. Content Strategy
9. Marketing Collateral
10. User Support Docs
11. Training Collaterals
12. Change Management
13. Social Media Assets
14. Digital Marketing Assets
15. Brand Playbook
16. Pricing Model Experiments
17. Market Positioning
18. Competitive Positioning
19. Ecosystem Map

A version of this appeared on www.ddiinnxx.com.

Product Management Thoughts & Ideas

7.
Can I Become a Good Product Manager?

AKA What does it take for me to try out Product Management?

Product Management is *very* simple. And perhaps that is why it is so **hard**.

There are three streams from which Product Managers arise:

- Design,
- Business, and
- Technology.

The key to being a good Product Manager is to rise from one of these positions of strength, and then immediately *lose* it.

Here is what I mean:

If a technologist takes up a product, they forever see it as a technical product and do not realize that they have to pay equal attention to its design and business. This is true for folks from design and business as well.

This, letting go, is where many smart folks fail.

If you are a technologist, do you have the willingness to give up being a technologist? If you can overcome that instinct and be cognizant of aspects of Design and Business, you will be an excellent Product Manager.

And this thought process is an important one if you want to be a successful founder!

A version of this appeared on www.ddiinnxx.com.

8.
Product Thinking = ProMA + Design + Business Model

Before we get started on Product Thinking, it is important for us to understand what a Product is.

A *Product is something that is the result of a process*[1].

Now, how does this apply to the software world? Let us see:

A *Product is something that is the result of a software process.*

This is better. However, is designing for humans (Experience Design, etc.) a software process? Not really. But, it is a distinct process in itself. So, an updated definition then:

A *Product is something that is the result of a design & software process.*

Better. However, I am of the opinion that a product without a business model is neither sustainable nor a solution.

So, let us add that to the mix.

A *Product is something that is the result of a design & software process and has a business model.*

OK, there! Now we can proceed to Product Thinking.

Product Thinking

Here it is in one diagram that was inspired by a Nikkel Blaase's post[2]:

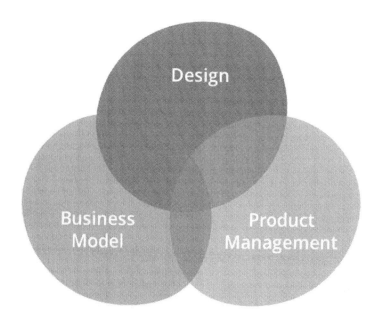

Figure 8-1: The Three-Circles of Product Thinking

Product Thinking is not the process of product creation itself. It is thinking of the product along with the whole ecosystem. The ecosystem is often a combination of:

- Target Audience
- Problem
- Strategy
- Vision, Objectives, Goals
- Features
- User Experience
- User Environment
- Process of Making
- Revenues

Based on the Product Management Canvas, we can define Product Thinking as:

Building on the value your customers will need to achieve business goals measured using related success and failure metrics with providing a well-designed experience using a well-defined go-to-market strategy and support.

Need v/s Will Need

You will notice, I said 'will need' rather than 'need'. A lot of innovations anticipate a need to create a new one. So, to acknowledge that, a 'will' has been added.

Platforms vs Channels

Platforms (backend, APIs, multi-tenancy, etc.) benefit from System Centric design (e.g., System Thinking) while Channels (apps, websites, devices, kiosks, etc.) which humans interact with benefit from User Centric design (e.g., Design Thinking).

What About Tech?

Doesn't technology figure in this at all? Technology is certainly very important but related to building the product. However, a lot of time gets spent on how a product gets built (and it involves other roles). This is why the focus is on other aspects to bring out Product Thinking.

One needs to be a strong technologist (and not necessarily a Developer) to be an effective Product Manager. This should ideally cover the Technology aspects.

A version of this appeared on www.ddiinnxx.com.

9.
Shuhari & Software Evolution

Shuhari (at times written as Shu-Ha-Ri), a Japanese learning system[1], roughly translates to "first learn, then detach, and finally transcend."

Another translation being, "Keeping, Breaking, and finally Independence[2]."

Shu / Learn or Keeping

In this stage, one

- Imbibes Rules,
- Follows Practices, and
- Understands Underlying Principles

Ha / Digress or Breaking

In this stage, one

- Understands Vision
- Bends Rules, and
- Questions Underlying Principles

Ri / Transcend or Independence

In this stage, one

- Upgrades Vision
- New Rules, and
- New Underlying Principles

It is often recommended for learning techniques and methodologies for software development[3].

In Context of Software Evolution

Your software is NOT the product.

When we put the Software in a context of a Problem or Opportunity, identify or establish an Ecosystem, find a Product — Market Fit, identify the Early Adopters, Value Prop for Early Adopters and decide on the Success & Failure Metrics — the software becomes a product.

Such products (like Commercial Off-the-shelf - COTS), however, focus on a process. It considers the more generic workflows and tries to be one software for most of the use-cases. Known to follow current established practices, it is the *Shu* stage of the evolution.

Adding to this an offering of Services enables better Adoption, Usability and helps build the Ecosystem. This, in the context of a business, is when a Product takes the form of a Solution.

*Solution = (Software + Service) * Context*

Solution is the *Ha* stage of evolution.

To transcend and reach the *Ri* stage, the solution should provide an *Evolutionary Business Model*. The new Business Model should potentially change the process itself and yet survive the disruption. This is the ultimate state of a software.

While Solution is beneficial for a client/customer, *Evolutionary Business Model* is beneficial for the organization itself. Only an organization that can sustain itself can continue to provide solutions to the clients.

Moto/The Purpose

As we transcendent, it is important to stay guided to the original purpose, the roots or the starting point. Shu-Ha-Ri is a system or a technique where the ultimate aim is to accomplish *the* purpose. Never lose sight of this.

Keep in mind the learning system: **Shu-Ha-Ri-Moto.**

A version of this appeared on www.ddiinnxx.com. There is a YouTube recording of a talk on the same topic available: http://bit.ly/2BTVgHO. A slide deck version of it is available on SlideShare: http://bit.ly/2svnGE4.

10.
SOFTWARE PRODUCT: A DEFINITION

Definitions matter. Not only do they enable common understanding, they sometimes ensure a particular behavior. Before going into what I mean by this, here is how I define a Software Product:

Software Product:

noun

noun: software product; plural noun: software products

> 1. something that is the result of a design & software process and has a business model.
>
> "I build software products for a living."

Read chapter 8 on how I arrived at this definition: Product Thinking = UX Design + ProMa + Business Model.

A version of this appeared on www.ddiinnxx.com.

11.
FIVE BUCKETS MODEL FOR PRODUCT MANAGEMENT

Inspired by The Five Competencies of User Experience Design[1], Five Buckets by Jonny Schneider (ThoughtWorks), and Five Buckets of Business Analysis by Jiangmei Kang (ThoughtWorks), I created a version for Product Management.

The 5 Buckets Model for Product Management

The Five Buckets is a model that describes the various capabilities of a Product Manager. This model lists out important capabilities and suggests them to be competent in a subset of capabilities based on what their focus or interest is.

The 5 Capabilities of Product Managers (ProMa) identified are:

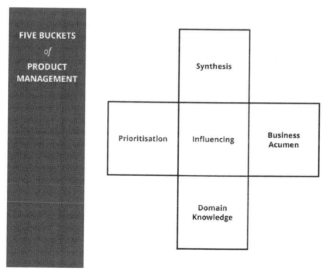

Figure 11-1: Five Buckets of Product Management

Influencing

- Rallying opinions around the Product value
- Active listening
- Evangelism
- Articulation of value
- Connect Business, Users, and Techies and be their advocate in Product decisions
- Establish common language
- Fill the communication gap
- Stakeholder engagement
- Problem-solving
- Decision making
- Conflicts resolution
- Jedi Mind Tricks[2] and Reality Distortion Field[3]
- Elevator pitches
- Quips, anecdotes, storytelling
- Personal leadership
- CxO level conversations

Synthesis

- Take inputs from various sources and synthesize them into one coherent vision
- Build Product Strategy
- Product Design, Innovation, and User Research while keeping inputs and behaviors in mind
- Work with Business Analysts, Experience Designers, Developers, stakeholders, contributors, builders, consumers, etc.

Prioritization

- Road mapping

- Track and Manage the Delivery Progress
- Manage and Prioritize the Product Backlog

Business Acumen

- Sustainability of the business based on the product
- Business case for ideas/product/innovations/incremental innovations
- Pricing
- Market scoping
- Market research
- Market size
- Market opportunity
- Product – Organization fit
- Product – Market fit

Domain Knowledge

- Ramp up at the needed pace to get sufficient Domain Knowledge
- SME or strong Design background or strong Development background

Some Key Thoughts

As with other versions, everyone has the combination of two or more capabilities, but nobody can be an expert in all five areas.

Influencing is a basic and key competency for ProMa to be effective.

Prioritization (road mapping, tracking, etc.) and Synthesis (gather inputs and make sense of conflicting demands) are key day-to-day activities of a ProMa guided by the right Business Acumen (business value of anything that crosses them).

For situations where Domain Knowledge is important, being an SME helps. Else, as a Generalist, ramping up to have sufficient knowledge of how domain works.

Based on the roles, here are some examples:

Ideator/Disruptor/Startup ProMa

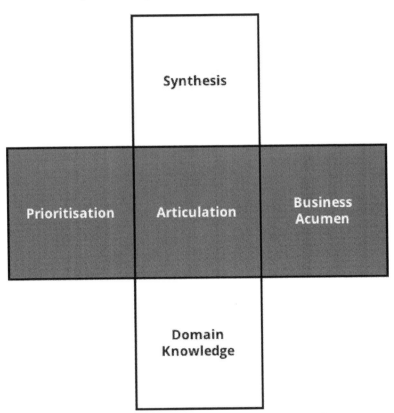

Figure 11-2: Five Buckets of Product Management for Ideator/Disruptor/Startup ProMa

Incremental Innovator / Enterprise ProMa

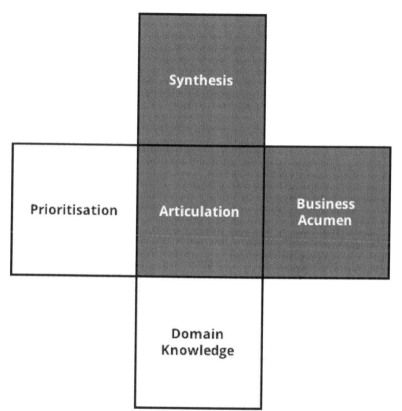

Figure 11-3: Five Buckets of Product Management for Incremental Innovator/Enterprise ProMa

Sustenance Stage Product ProMa

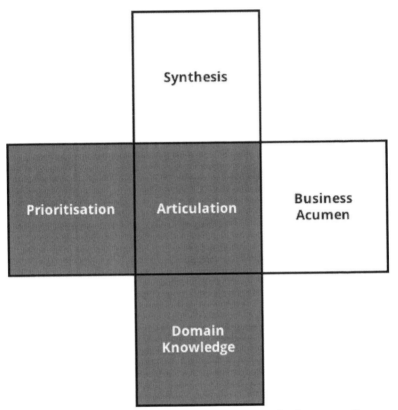

Figure 11-4: Five Buckets of Product Management for Sustenance Stage Product ProMa

Domain Specific Product ProMa

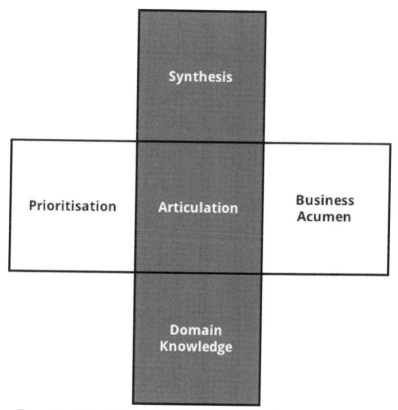

Figure 11-5: Five Buckets of Product Management for Domain-Specific Product ProMa

A version of this appeared on www.ddiinnxx.com. There are YouTube recordings of talks on the same subject available: http://bit.ly/2nT2hjs and http://bit.ly/2G4XiTg. Slide deck versions of respective talks are available on SlideShare: http://bit.ly/2o0zl8n and http://bit.ly/2Emj4pr. A slide deck version of it is available on SlideShare: http://bit.ly/2ElPkVw.

12.
The Product Sociologist

"A general definition of sociology is the systematic study of human society, culture, and relationships on a group level. So, basically, sociology looks at the 'big picture' on the group level."[1]

"Sociology is the study of human social relationships and institutions."[2]

"Sociology is the study of social behavior or society, including its origins, development, organization, networks, and institutions."[3]

"No product is an island." (paraphrasing[4] *John Donne*[5]*)*

Sociology, to me, is the study of human interaction with one another, the relationships that develop, how these relationships form groups, how these groups interact with each other, etc.

As Product Managers, we should always be aware of the 'nature' of our product. Almost create an anthropomorphised version of it. We should always be aware of how it interacts with other products and what sort of grouping it forms with other products and the ecosystem that comes up around it.

This, to me, is very important as we need to know how our product is doing out there in the wild world and how users are making it interact with other products we may not even be aware of.

As Product Managers, we should be thinking and acting as *Product Sociologists*.

Let me take Twitter as an example. It has a color, an icon, and a look-feel. You know the twitter icon on the screen of your phone amidst other apps. You know you can register or sign-in using Twitter. You can tweet a passage in a book reader without leaving the book reader. You can promote your T-Shirt design on Twitter. You can start a Digital Media agency that helps brands build an image using Twitter. You can use other products that tell you what your social worth is based on your followers.

If you are a ProMa at Twitter, will you just look at the product you are responsible for, or will you step back and understand the influence your product has on various ways Twitter exists or its place in the current digital landscape?

Once the product is seen as an entity that interacts with other entities, the following becomes obvious: look at our product as an entity in itself.

For a software product, it is easy to know how it was built, the architecture, current bugs, and any intricate detail. Most of the time, the Product Manager is part of the building process.

However, Product Managers should be able to abstract all this out and look at the product in its entirety and as atomic. That the product is sufficient. That the product can stand on its own. Once we do that, a crash, APIs, certain bug-feature, etc., describe the nature and quirkiness of a product. How the product lends itself to be easily integrated to others describes the sociability of the product. All these become part of the product's personality.

As Product Managers, we should also be thinking and acting as *Product Psychologists*.

And there is at least one role model! **Susan Calvin,** the famous Robopsychologist from Issac Asimov's Robot series[6]!

A version of this appeared on www.ddiinnxx.com.

13.
ARE NON-TECHNICAL PRODUCT MANAGERS BECOMING IRRELEVANT?

There are three streams from which Product Managers arise:

- Design,
- Business, and
- Technology.

The key to being a good ProMa is to rise from one of these positions of strength, and then immediately *lose* it. I have talked about it in chapter 7

So, if a technologist takes up a product, they should not only see it as a technical problem; they should pay equal attention to its design and business.

If you are a technologist, are you willing to give up being a technologist? If you can overcome that instinct and be cognizant of aspects of Design and Business, you will be an excellent Product Manager.

So, as long as you know the business, domain or design, you have no fear of being irrelevant.

A version of this appeared on www.ddiinnxx.com.

14.
PRODUCT ENTREPRENEURSHIP V/S PRODUCT MANAGEMENT

"So, a Product Manager is like a Project Manager for a Product?"

"Isn't Management all about keeping things running?"

"Do I need an MBA to be a Product Manager?"

"I don't want to be a Manager."

"Nobody likes Managers."

Does the term Product Management reflect the breadth, creativity and responsibility? The more I ask, the more I realize that it does not.

A lot of this may be due to the growing number of 'Leader v/s Manager' comparisons on LinkedIn and lack of clarity on the difference between a Project Manager and a Product Manager.

Anyway, does it matter? If the colloquial meaning does not match the textbook meaning, should it concern us? Maybe yes, maybe no.

However, given the evolution of Products and how we interact with them, it is time for a reimagining. And what better way to start than to look for the right name?

Product Management

Let us look at the life of a product. This is how the RACI matrix for a Product Manager is perceived to look like for each phase:

Phase	Product Manager
Opportunity	–
Strategy	–
Discovery	Consulted
Define	Responsible
Design	Responsible
Deliver	Informed
Sustain	Accountable
Sunset	Informed

Table 14-1: Product Manager's RACI

Product Entrepreneur

The role of a Product Entrepreneur can be used to describe the real breadth of the scope of work that makes a product possible.

This is how the RACI matrix for a Product Entrepreneur is perceived to look like for each phase:

Phase	Product Manager	Product Entrepreneur
Opportunity	–	Consulted
Strategy	–	Consulted
Discovery	Consulted	Responsible

Define	Responsible	Responsible
Design	Responsible	Responsible
Deliver	Informed	Informed
Sustain	Accountable	Accountable
Sunset	Informed	Accountable

Table 14-2: Product Entrepreneur's RACI

A Product Entrepreneur may be a better term for the breadth of work. The adoption of this may be a whole different story.

While it is easier to be a Product Entrepreneur in a startup or small enterprise, the real challenge is being an effective one in a large enterprise. The Product Entrepreneur will have to rise with courage in responsibility and visibility to be on the table when opportunities are being assessed and strategies are being devised.

As my colleague, Nagarjun Kandukuru, often says, "A ProMa's role is hard to nail. That may be one of its charms and challenges."

A version of this appeared on www.ddiinnxx.com.

15.
WATERFALL VS AGILE: AN AGE-OLD BATTLE

Charvaka (no relation) is the ancient school of Indian materialism. Charvaka holds direct perception, empiricism, conditional inference as proper sources of knowledge and embraces philosophical skepticism.[1]

It is generally held that inference leads to knowledge. The Inference can be drawn based on previous knowledge and one or more observations. A typical example is a phrase like: where there's smoke, there's fire.

However, inference can be wrong as we can't know all possible conditions, make all observations, and clarify all possible premises. We know only what we observe.

Sounds familiar?

All conditions, all observations, all premises gathered as requirements, upfront! That's the Waterfall Model.

Perception knowledge is what your 5 senses tell your mind here & now.

It is not possible to know all conditions, all observations, all premises, and all requirements upfront! All we know is what we can observe and we base our decisions on those observations.

Sounds familiar?

That's Lean + Agile!

Seems Lean + Agile has been winning over Waterfall since 600 BCE!

A version of this appeared on www.ddiinnxx.com. A slide deck version of it is available on SlideShare: http://bit.ly/2EXZXPm.

16.
PRODUCT DEVELOPMENT & THE SCIENTIFIC PROCESS

Early Days

Francis Bacon, a 1500 CE philosopher, scientist, and lawyer came up with what can be called the first enunciation of the Scientific Process.

He established a three-step process[1]:

- Make observations to produce facts
- Generalize facts to form axioms
- Gather data to establish it

This process gets repeated to build an increasingly complex body of knowledge.

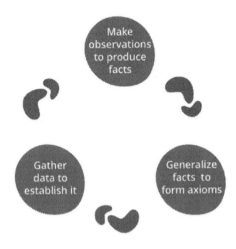

Figure 16-1: Scientific Process by Francis Bacon

Generalize the facts to form axioms is analogous to Build. *Gather data to establish it* is analogous to Measure. And, finally, *make observations to produce facts* is analogous to Learn.

Looks familiar?

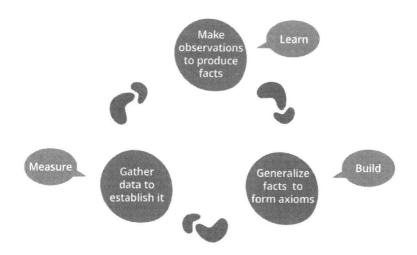

Figure 16-2: Build-Measure-Learn by Francis Bacon

Descartes, a 1600 CE philosopher, scientist, mathematician proposed a similar approach.

Start with a Hypotheses. Then use Deduction to make a Prediction. Then make Observations to Test the Prediction. Finally, use Induction to make and produce a fact.

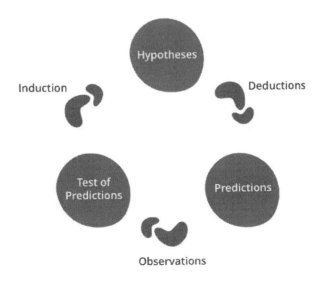

Figure 16-3: Scientific Process by René Descartes

Do these remind you of something?

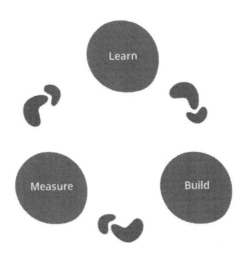

Figure 16-4: Build-Measure-Learn

Turns out, Build-Measure-Learn has been around and winning since 1500 CE!

Modern Scientific Process

Wikipedia user, ArchonMagnus, has a great representation of the Scientific Method as an Ongoing Process[2].

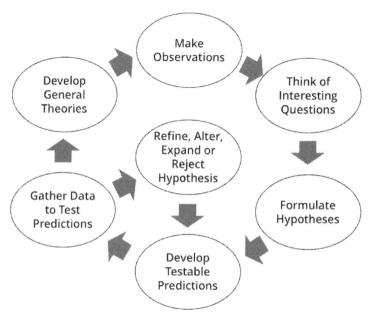

Figure 16-5: ArchonMagnus' Modern Scientific Process

This maps to the Product process very well. The flow that follows can be:

Make Observations

- Identify Need, Pain-points
- Spot Opportunities.

Think of Interesting Questions

Use techniques like:

- The 5 Whys - 5 Whys is an iterative interrogative technique used to explore the cause-and-effect relationships underlying a particular problem.[3]

- 4W1H - "Where, when, what, who and how!"[4]

- HEART - "Happiness, Engagement, Adoption, Retention and Task. A framework for user-centered metrics, as well as a process for mapping product goals to the Success of metrics."[5]

- Secondary Research - Also known as desk research and it involves the summary, collation and/or synthesis of existing research rather than primary research, in which data are collected from, for example, research subjects or experiments.[6]

Formulate Hypotheses

- User Research
- Wireframes
- MVP
- Biz Models

Develop Testable Predictions

- Development
- Metrics
- Go-To-Market

Gather Data to Test Predictions

- Analytics

- Data Science
- User Research

Refine, Alter, Expand or Reject Hypothesis

Develop General Theories

- Release to market
- Dominate the market

The analogous Product development process becomes:

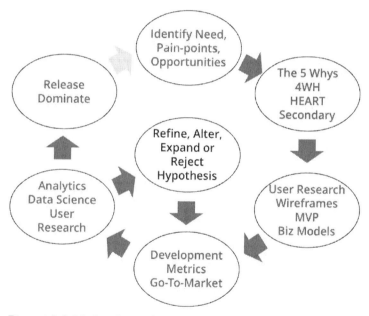

Figure 16-6: Modern Scientific Process as Product Development Process

Turns out the Design Process is the same as the Product Process and the Scientific Process.

We come across many frameworks, charts, '10 Things' articles on Startups, Product Development, etc. Some even exist in this book.

They are all essentially customization & contextualization of existing wisdom.

A version of this appeared on www.ddiinnxx.com. A slide deck version of it is available on SlideShare: http://bit.ly/2EXZXPm.

17.
IT TAKES A VILLAGE

In Product Development & Scientific Process, I discussed how the product development process mimics the scientific process.

What the process implies is that it takes a village to build a product. We often hear about the charismatic founder or the star developers. The story of other contributors does not get told that often.

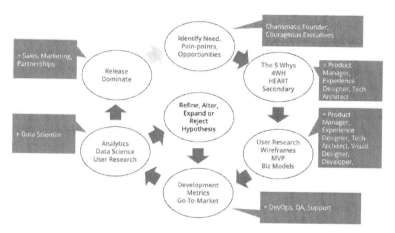

Figure 17-1: Actors in Modern Product Development Process

Specific roles become critical at various stages and join the village in moving the product forward.

A version of this appeared on www.ddiinnxx.com. A slide deck version of it is available on SlideShare: http://bit.ly/2EXZXPm.

18.
7 REASONS WHY YOUR PRODUCT WILL FAIL

Seven things your users may be thinking that will cause your product to fail:

1. **"I don't like it."**

   "A lot of times, people don't know what they want until you show it to them.[1]"

   - Steve Jobs

To avoid this, try techniques like Rapid Prototyping and Wireframing to get the feedback early. Sometimes, using analogies that reference known products (X of Y for Z) helps.

2. **"I don't even want it."**

   There are around 5M software products on the market.

At the intersection of what the users want, what your product does well, and what other software does not do well lies the success of your product.

To find that, try techniques like Gap Analysis, USP identification, and formal Product Definition. Share it with target customers early and seek feedback. This will also ensure that your product is neither ahead of its time, nor too late to the market.

3. "I don't even know how to use it."

> *"The adult public's taste is not necessarily ready to accept the logical solutions to their requirements if the solution implies too vast a departure from what they have been conditioned into accepting as the norm.[2]"*
>
> *- Raymond Loewy ('The Man Who Shaped America', 'The Father of Streamlining', and 'The Father of Industrial Design'.)*

You will hear, "the user should instinctively know how to use the product", a lot. There is no way to know other than by trying. Try till the right interface/design is discovered.

Techniques like Habit Building and building right User Interfaces used by Experience Designers can help you build something very usable.

4. "I am happy with what I have."

> *People are not lazy. They just love inertia. Thus, users move to a new product if the existing one is either badly broken or the new product is kind of amazing.*

Empathy Maps and Product Migration plans can help you help users identify gaps and move to your product. Product Marketing can help you amplify the message and reach the right set of prospective users.

Apple's 'Switch'[3] and 'I'm a Mac I'm a PC'[4] ad campaigns are excellent examples.

5. "I don't want to pay for it."

> *The amount most people are willing to pay for an app is $0—until they've actually downloaded it.*

Working on getting your Product Pricing right using User Research and building robust Business Models can help you convert users into customers. There are few good articles on common business models to help you find the right one[5].

6. "No one else is using it."

> *Expert social proof, Celebrity Social Proof, User Social Proof, 'Wisdom of the Crowds' Social Proof and 'Wisdom of Your Friends' Social Proof matters.*

Your Go-To-Market, Product Marketing, and Product Branding should allow for Social proof to be enabled and communicated. Easy posting to social media networks, badges, user ranking, top posters, reviews, etc., are commonly used methods.

7. "I don't trust it."

> *"We want to build a website where people publicly post pictures of their bedrooms and bathrooms. And then, over the Internet, they're going to invite complete strangers to come sleep in their homes. It's going to be huge![6]"*
>
> *- Joe Gebbia on AirBnB*

Product Support and Product Reviews establish trust especially when it lays bare the pros and cons. These and other aspects of User Psychology can help establish trust with your users.

While this leans heavily towards B2C products, a lot of these lessons are applicable for B2B products too.

A version of this appeared on www.ddiinnxx.com. A slide deck version of it is available on SlideShare: http://bit.ly/2nVjxEB.

19.
MVP OF A DATA PLATFORM

One approach to building an MVP for a Data Platform is to identify a thin vertical slice business value and implement it. You then proceed to do the same for another business value till the whole platform is built. This is analogous to Strangler Approach[1] to re-writing an existing critical system.

However, using this approach as-is runs the risk of creating a platform that was too close to the first business process this platform served and tied to the relevant data sources.

A way to mitigate this is to focus on providing a minimal set of capabilities that will be very useful for the one business process so they will invest in making changes in their applications to benefit from the platform.

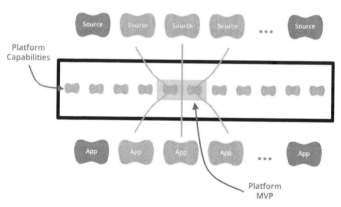

Figure 19-1: MVP of a Data Platform

However, those minimal set of capabilities should be sufficiently useful for at least one or more other business processes. The platform should be useful enough for the other two so they will surely invest enough time with teams building the platform to discuss the requirements of the business process and possibly find what is being delivered as MVP useful.

Inception (discussed in various chapters earlier), is a good time to look for a primary business process and say two more other processes. It is always good to prioritize business processes that deliver higher business value over technical value. You will find it easy to explain the value of investing in a Data Platform when a business value to the end client is being delivered that something that covers technical-debt or make operations more efficient.

I refer to this approach to MVP as an hour-glass approach: broad on top covering few business processes, narrow in middle in form of minimal capability and broad at the bottom covering broader data sources.

This is a previously unpublished chapter.

Entrepreneurship

20.
One Degree of Separation

Startups are exciting

Everyone believes so. But what is so exciting about a Startup? You can almost use this question as a Rorschach Test to find out what is lacking in their career now.

Everyone has something they feel/think is great about startups: the transparency, lack of bureaucracy, connect with client, knowledge about vital stats of an org, flat hierarchy, ability to control your own fate within the org, see effects of your contribution, struggle to find answers for basic questions like how the org will make money, the fact that we own the problem and not blame others, and so on and so forth.

The Other Side

While we tend to get enamored by the opportunities startups throw at us, the other side is hardly discussed. Something that all entrepreneurs surrender to live through and ultimately succumb to. But that is a discussion for another day.

The One-Degree Separation

One thing that startups offer (and is the root cause of many things exciting about it) is that founders and early employees are just one degree away from the consequences of their work/decision.

They know revenue generated, cost incurred, potential and compromises, success first hand, and what product/decision caused that.

There is no alienation from the consequences of the product they produce.

So What?

This is one thing large Enterprises and Software Services companies specially can adopt/imbibe from startups world:

One Degree of Separation from the consequences of our work.

Once we are aware of the consequences of our work, finding, owning and solving problems will be self-motivated. If we are *not* aware, we will continue to be a cog in the wheel that is unaware of its importance.

Also, Software Services companies work with clients on a product/project. They are inherently always few degrees away from the consequences of their work. At times, the department they work with (example Engineering), itself, is a few degrees away from the department which faces the final consequences of the work (example Support).

So This Means?

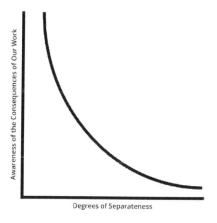

Figure 20-1: Awareness of Consequences vis-à-vis Degrees of Separation

With each degree of separation, the context, sense-of-ownership, and the awareness for value delivered decreases exponentially.

So, What Next?

In order to adopt/imbibe this key lesson, the challenge is on how to be one degree separate from the consequences of the work. That can be best answered by the organization itself.

A version of this appeared on www.ddiinnxx.com.

21.
THE MOST MEMORABLE OF TEAMS

Six Characteristics of an Effective and Memorable Team

A few weeks ago, I was at an off-site meeting. As part of the warm-up exercise, all attendees were asked to talk about their most memorable team experience.

As I took notes, a pattern began to emerge. The following characteristics came up again and again:

- Laser focus on execution
- Coming together of different personalities
- Lack of clear direction
- Do or Die situations
- There to create something
- Knew their strengths and limitations

So, it looks like if diversity, ambiguity on how to achieve the goals, focus, do/die, clear purpose for the team and team members are present, it is a memorable experience.

One more thing to note: not all projects were a success. The products/projects may have failed, but the participants felt the teams were at their possible best.

This raises some interesting questions:

If such conditions are created, will any team become highly effective? Or, is this non-commutative?

A version of this appeared on www.ddiinnxx.com.

22.
DIRTY-WORK GROUP

Negative emotions are stronger than positive ones and often we know clearly what we do not want to do rather than knowing what we want to do.

The Dirty-work group is based on this hypothesis.

So, let us put it up as an example. Your wife does not enjoy driving. You do not enjoy sitting idle in the car. Thus, you drive and she navigates. What a happy dirty-work group you are!

Introduction

First, what is a dirty-work? It is a job which a person can do but doesn't like to do, even if they are good at it. So much so that the person would rather do any other job, even if it's a job he/she is not too good at.

A dirty-work group is a small heterogeneous group in which each does not have to do their dirty work because one person's dirty-work is not so for someone else in the group. This has to be cyclic.

The Advantage

Besides helping to form a team, the process is useful in:

- Identifying the strength and weakness of team members
- Identifying weakness that is not covered by another team member and thus identifying a weak link
- It is a great team-work promoting method where one gets to openly talk about their pet peeves

- It provides team structure, work distribution, and robustness of the team

An Entrepreneurial Tool

Don't let your lack of ability to do it stop you from doing what you want to do.

Let us face it. Either we have all the talent needed to pull off an idea or we do not have all the talent to pull off the idea. Should this lack of talent stop us from going ahead and following the idea?

Conventional wisdom says, if you can't do it, you won't be able to do it. So forget it.

Shouldn't we?

In a modern market, a businessman should have multiple capabilities to survive. Not every entrepreneur can hire accountants, financial advisors, lawyers, and technical experts for advice. They start with limited resources and consultants don't come cheap.

All entrepreneurs have one common quality — they are good at multiple tasks. If a successful entrepreneur was good at computers, sure there was at least one more field which the entrepreneur had a "natural knack" for. Maybe marketing, finance or any other area that helped in converting an 'idea' into a business reality.

However, at times, either that is not sufficient or there may be a lack of 'natural knack'. It can discourage an entrepreneur into inaction. A Dirty-Work Group model can be a good approach to walk away unscathed from all these problems.

A version of this appeared on www.ddiinnxx.com.

23.
ARE STARTUPS AN MVP FOR MASLOW'S HIERARCHY?

What's an MVP?

An MVP has features that are just enough to prove a value and justify continued development.

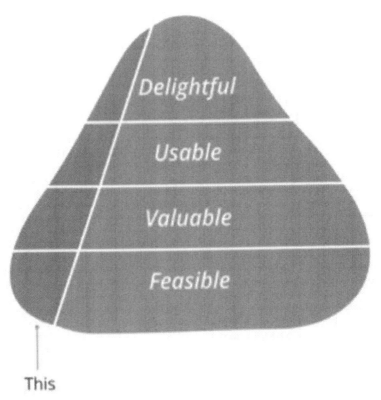

Figure 23-1: MVP from Lean Enterprise by Jez Humble, Joanne Molesky and Barry O'Reilly

We have all seen this image[1]. The MVP cuts across the value hierarchy and delivers a bit of each level.

What's Maslow's Hierarchy of Needs?

Maslow's hierarchy of needs[2] is a motivational theory in psychology that comprises of a five-tier model of human needs, often depicted as hierarchical levels within a pyramid.

Figure 23-2: Maslow's Hierarchy of Needs

We have all seen this. The theory states that people are motivated to achieve certain needs, and that some needs take precedence over others. Once that level is fulfilled, the next level up is what motivates us, and so on.

There are few criticisms of this theory and changes to be made. One being that in real life, these are not strictly hierarchies.

Startups and Maslow's Hierarchy

One reason why startup excites us is that in one go, it satisfies each of these needs. A la how the MVP cuts across the value hierarchy and delivers a bit of each level.

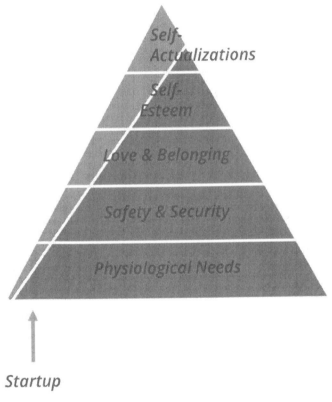

Figure 23-3: Startups and Maslow's Hierarchy

While they may not pay a lot, the basic needs are covered. There is a strong sense of belongingness to the startup and one other. The awe and aura of being an entrepreneur boosts the esteem. Finally, the opportunity to create a business or a brand makes a difference to the ultimate realization of personal potential.

Conclusion

Startups represent that thin vertical slice across Maslow Hierarchy making it an MVP for it. That explains the fascination with it. This insight can be used by other orgs to create avenues for employees to have the same experience with leaving to start a startup.

A version of this appeared on www.ddiinnxx.com.

24.
OUR CHILDREN AND THE DIGITAL FUTURE

Why This?

As Founder of Gungroo Software and the creator of Roo Kids App, an Instant Messaging app for children where parents have access to the contacts and always know who the kid is chatting with, this area is of immense interest to me.

Easing Children into Real World

As automobiles started to become commonplace on the roads, parents started teaching their children to cross a road effectively. Our schools started talking about safety habits around the roads. School buses added STOP signs, so traffic could give way to a kid crossing the road.

The Digital Future

A digital future is inevitable and some argue that we are already there. As the 4th Industrial Revolution rolls in, how do we educate and ease our kids into such a world?

Not Just The Parents

No, it is not the responsibility of the parents alone. It is everybody's concern. Especially those who are involved in the creation of products (including startup founders who are re-inventing the world). Will it be easy for kids to step into this re-invented world? Or, will they stumble and fall prey to it?

A Manifesto For Children Inclusive Digital Future

We (Startup Founders, Product Managers, Product Designers, Product Business Managers, and Technologists) are developing products and helping others do it while keeping children in mind.

Through this work, we have come to value:

Products that provide an overlap of safety oversight & digital access over products that are command-control tools or promote digital ignorance.

[Rather than building products that isolate tech or isolate kids, we will build products that 1/ expose enough for kids to learn & explore, and 2/ provide tools to provide sufficient oversight to maintain safety.]

Products that consider incidental or accidental use by children over products that assume otherwise.

[Never assume that a child will not incidentally or accidentally access our product. Have we considered that in our design, implementation, and usage guidelines? Responsibility towards children is not restricted to products created for children.]

Products that respect individuality, intelligence, and privacy of a child over products that make stereotypic generalization like age ranges, gender, etc.

[Standardization makes sense when we can't customize at scale. Digital products allow for customization and personalization on a large scale. Digital products should adapt to a child and present a match without violating privacy and should also provide for sufficient anonymity. Privacy also includes providing children with enough space where they are assured privacy in the context of parents too but always within a safe space.]

That is, while there was value in the items on the right in early days of digital evolution, we value the items on the left more.

Note: This approach and format is inspired by the Manifesto for Agile Software Development[1].

A version of this appeared on www.ddiinnxx.com.

25.
STARTUP HIRING TIPS – THE GOLDEN RULE

Take a long time to hire, but if needed, let go very fast.

Hiring key members of a team is the single most crucial decision a founder makes. So, hiring should be done right, and if things do not turn out well, let go early. It is best for your startup and the person involved.

Hiring in Startups

Many articles have been written on this. But here are my top 2 suggestions:

<u>More Interview Sessions per Candidate Is Good</u>

Make sure that the candidate is interviewed by as many people in your startup and possibly outsiders whom you trust. Make sure this group is diverse in their function and experience.

<u>360-Degree Interview Is Good</u>

If the candidate is coming at a senior position and will lead a team that is already part of the startup journey, a 360-degree interview is essential.

"People are good. It is the matching that can be good or bad."

If your existing team does not feel the candidate will help them leap forward and higher, you may end up losing them eventually. The 360-degree feedback will help you catch such issues before the candidate is hired.

Letting Go in Startups

Sometimes, we do make mistakes and end up with a wrong person-role match. Remember my match up rule:

"People are good. It is the matching that can be good or bad."

<u>'I Can Fix' This Is Bad</u>

If startups end up in a situation of a wrong hire, I have seen smart leaders make the same mistake: they think they can fix it. This causes the following issues:

- Discontent among performers that you are paying too much attention to a non-performer,
- Discontent among those affected that you care more about a wrong hire than those who are delivering, and
- Sense of personal failure in the hire that in spite of all the support, he/she cannot deliver.

There is no point fighting a battle in which there will be no winners — your startup will lose most.

<u>'Let Me Help You Move On' Is Good</u>

Help the wrong hire find a better fit. This will ensure you:

- Have not burnt bridges with a smart person,
- You will maintain a strong relationship that you can use in a future hire where there is a better match, and
- Your existing team will feel inspired that you never abandon anyone.

A version of this appeared on www.ddiinnxx.com.

26.
FAILING SINCE 2012

Failing. Not failed!

We are failing every day, and this is the difference with a startup. It is a daily struggle to not be part of the '90% who failed'.

I started in 2012 and it has been quite a journey launching Roo Kids Chat App. It is always a right time to look back and revisit the lessons learned, for the journey is not over yet.

• • •

Get Set, Go – The First Few Months in 2012

Gungroo was built with the vision of a safe and secure messaging for kids. That is how we started, and that is what we are today. But somewhere along the way …

Private Family Network

The product started as a private network for families where an admin could allow kids' logins to be created (without an email) and family members joining using their email addresses.

Instead of 1, Gungroo needed 2 passwords for a user to login. This was a crazy idea. The reason was simple: people like to pick bad passwords. They always do. Just by making it 2 passwords, we were increasing safety by order. 'hello123' and 'password123' are bad passwords. But 'hello123password123' is a whole different level.

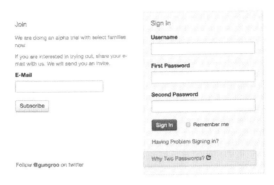

Figure 26-1: Two Password Login

But, no parent came. Not even the parents who liked the idea and wanted to jump on such a product. Was it the very plain looking UI, the 2 passwords thing (it did confuse people and our UX guy disapproved of it), or what was it? But from the number of times I heard, 'Yes, I will create an account and set up soon', it was obvious: our product needed a lot of setup time.

We did notice that friends whose workplaces had banned Facebook were using Gungroo a lot. No one in IT knew about Gungroo and they used it for all intra-office gossip.

Moderated Client for Gmail

We moved on to add the next planned feature: a moderated client for Gmail. The way it worked was that a parent would create a Gmail account for the kid using the parent's real info. They never share the password with the kid. Then they set up Gmail on Gungroo. When an email arrived in Gmail's inbox, Gungroo imported it using IMAP, sent to parent, had the parent inspect it, approved it and then the kid gets it in his/her inbox on Gungroo. And vice versa for sending. Cool?

And, no parent came. Not even the parents who liked the idea and wanted to jump on such a product. Was it the very plain looking UI, the need to approve each and every message, email not being as hot as social media, or what was it? But from the number of times I heard, 'Yes, I will create an account and set up soon', it was obvious: now our product needed even more setup time.

Moderated Client for Facebook

We moved on to add the next planned feature: a moderated client for Facebook. The way it worked was that a parent would allow Gungroo's Facebook app to read and write on their wall.

When kids used Gungroo's interface to post on Facebook, it was sent to the parent for approval, and on approval, it was posted to the parent's wall on Facebook via Gungroo's Facebook App. All likes and comments on that post were imported to Gungroo and shown to the kid.

Thus, Gungroo acted as a safe and moderated client to Facebook. Cool!?

Guess what, no parent came. Not even the parents who liked the idea and wanted to jump on such a product. Was it the very plain looking UI, the need to approve each and every message, the right audience not knowing about the product, or what was it? But from the number of times I heard, 'Yes, that is a great idea', it was obvious: our product was targeting the wrong set of people.

Users vs Customers

Safe Web for Your Kid

Private Family Network   Parental Guidance   Messaging   Access Social Networks

Figure 26-2: Safe Web Solutions from Gungroo Highlighted on Home Page

This is when I realized why making products for kids is considered tough. The users are the kids and they have their own thing going. The customers who will pay for it are parents, and they have their own preferences. There was no way we could balance the two and make both happy. We had to bet on the parents. Parents are busy and have a whole world of worries to keep them busy. Setting up Gungroo was something that had to be done as soon as …

We decided to bet on kids instead. If kids like something enough, they will find a way for their parents to pay for it. This was not a space where a parent could influence the kid much anyway. The only space where parents can strongly influence their kids is in education. No wonder Edutech does so much better.

• • •

When The Going Get Tough (Up To 2013)

The last few months of 2012 and all of 2013 saw us churn out products at an alarming rate.

Curated YouTube Content

Once we decided we would focus on kids (rather than parents), we started by adding videos. Our staff selected these videos and channels. Parents could suggest videos, and they would go live once approved by our staff.

This led to something that was not new for us: Parents liking the idea. 'Finally, there is a site where I can feel assured that the videos my kid is watching are safe.'

But this also led to something that was totally new for us: Kids started using our site. Our traffic grew! And we started to get the cooperation of the parents!

Kids Games

We started putting up games on Gungroo.com. Many of these we sourced from sites like girlsgogames.com. Some like Kill My Time, Diwali Blast, Noisy Nathu, etc., were built in-house. This section did very well.

Sketching Apps – My Sketch Roo and Trace My Pix

The idea of a sketching app came in a company meeting where we were brainstorming on what next. Once the idea was on the floor, everyone latched onto it. This was all we discussed in the rest of the meeting.

My Sketch Roo was an HTML5 Canvas based app where one could draw and save a sketch. The sketch would show up in the public gallery once our staff approved it.

Soon we had kids making sketches and saving them in their profile on Gungroo.com. Not only were we fun as a product, we were also interactive and had user-generated content. Over 20K sketches have been made using this app.

Then we built a variant of this web app where you upload an image and sketch over it to create a pretty accurate sketch. We called it 'Trace My Pix'.

As the usage grew, we noticed that parents were sharing the sketches on Facebook (Twitter wasn't that popular). Pretty soon, Facebook became a critical part of spreading the content and getting more users.

However, kids were not our only users. Grown-ups started using the apps a lot. The idea of sketching appealed to both grown-ups and kids. There was no real way to stop grown-ups from using it.

The product, rather than the audience we wanted to target, was defining us. "Let us embrace this and see how far we can pull it." That is when we thought of creating a kid's version and a grown-up version.

My Sketch Roo as Facebook App

We created Facebook apps of both My Sketch Roo and Trace My Pix.

On Gungroo.com, which we built for kids, we were seeing grown-ups use our app to make sketches. On Facebook Apps, which we built for grown-ups, we started seeing kids use our app to make sketches!

Kids in India were on Facebook. We had heard about it. But we were starting to see it for real now.

Art Contests

You make a sketch, and you share it. What next? We decided to hold regular sketching competitions. For every contest, we used to pick a theme and awarded two prizes. One prize went to the entry with the most number of Likes + Tweets + Up Votes and the other prize went to staff's choice.

The logic was simple. The more Likes, Tweets and Up Votes we get, the more people know about us, and we get more traffic. But these entries may not always be the best. So, the staff picked the one we thought was the best. A combination of quantity and quality.

Let Teen Be

As we came to terms with the presence of kids on Facebook, we realized that a lot of time this was happening, it was with the full knowledge of the parents. So, we decided to create a dashboard for parents of teens on Facebook.

We were worried it might come across as a *creepy* app meant for 'helicopter parents[1]'. So, we presented it as minimal monitoring by parents. Key aspects being: keeping track of who the friends are and what the teen is posting with public visibility. The parent had to send a request to the teen and the teen had to allow the parent's request for this dashboard to work. This helped in establishing a level of trust with the teen.

We even sent out a press release that got some interesting write-ups. This app became very popular.

My Public Profile

In early 2013, many grownups were not very Facebook savvy; Facebook hadn't figured out Privacy well, and users were never sure what was visible on their public profile.

We got a couple of queries asking if there was a way for a parent to know what was visible on their own public profile.

We created a variant called My Public Profile. This showed the pictures and posts that were visible to the public. We showed it for the last 7 days. To see beyond 7 days, the user had to invite 10 more friends to use the app. Once 10 friends started using the app, the user could see public posts from the time the profile was created on Facebook. Due to this in-built virality, this app became very popular.

All our vitals were indicating good progress. Except one: Revenue. It was time to sit down and think about earning revenue. As they say, fund raised is not same as revenue generated.

War of Fascinating Galaxies

I like writing short stories. I even authored two collections called The Murmurs of the Dawn and Absolute and None. So, when it came to creating a real-world product, I decided to fall back on something I really enjoyed: Sci-fi and Physics.

Talking to parents and other founders, I realized that here in India, people prefer to pay for something tangible. E.g., they may use an online service, but it will be to buy something tangible like a book, dress or a ticket. So, we decided to make something tangible for the kids.

I used to hang around in toy stores and try to figure out what products sell most.

And I had to do this without seeming like a creep.

It was User v/s Customer play out all over again. This time, our focus was on the users. It was obvious to us within a week of these field trips that Trading Cards were big. Kids loved them and could not get enough of them. They came in small packages, were easy to make, and not so expensive that parents will think thrice (they always think twice before buying anything).

So, we created a sci-fi backstory and some interesting characters. We created a set of trading cards in which 40% of the cards were about the characters from our sci-fi backstory, and 60% were about cool Physics stuff. See what we did there? Balance Users and Customers. We talked about the physics stuff to the parents. We talked about characters and sci-fi to the kids. They loved it, and the kids absorbed the physics stuff too.

We created games that could be played using these cards and made videos demonstrating those games[2][3]. Though it was all fun and games, there was also some serious learning happening.

These cards sold like proverbial hotcakes. We sold them at fairs, apartments, etc. If a kid played any of the card games with us for even just 30 seconds, they would end up buying it!

But, we could not replicate this success online. We could never sell them in quantities we would have loved to, without them being an online hit. And we just could not crack that.

Still, this was our biggest revenue generating product.

We recently added images from these trading cards as stickers in Roo Kids. You can read part of the backstory here[4].

Blog For Parents

As the popularity grew, we were seeing some interest from brands for advertising. These brands wanted to advertise to parents. But our site was for kids, and we did not want to show ads. Also, it was tough to get ads going in Facebook Apps. So, we decided to add a blog section with content for parents.

We were learning a lot about parenting and what kids liked. So, we started writing articles around our learnings. We also added articles that were 'Top 10' like of lists, etc.

We started getting requests for review by founders who were creating apps for kids. We decided to do it for free. This turned out to be a blessing in disguise for the Roo Kids app. Without having to do any outreach, all kids app creators were finding us and contacting us.

We were getting to know what sorts of apps were being created and how well they were doing. This became a very important learning and motivation for creating the Roo Kids app.

Chasing Audience

Almost till the end of 2013, we churned out products & pivoted at a rate of one every 2 months. We blindly went where we got more users, registrations, interactions, page views, etc.

We ended up with 23 products. And now it was time to consolidate and refine.

. . .

The First Purge (Early 2014)

23

Our first one and a half year of the journey was full of experiments, twists, turns, pivots, and blind chase. This resulted in *23* products, each a startup idea in itself.

It was clear that we could not do it all and had to drop the ones that were digressions, had no future, or just could not be maintained by our small team.

Team Size

One thing that I have not talked about is our team size. Mostly by intent and at times by coincidence, the team size has always been 4, including me. When one left, another joined in, and the team size always remained the same.

It was quite a feat for a team of 4 to create 23 products in 1.5 years. But we had to drop some if this small team had to maintain products and keep the quality high.

Purge Begins

We listed out all the products and variants and assigned them a score based on the following factors:

1. *Virality*: We defined virality as growth driven by a user where they had to bring other users to the product or the platform for it to be of use. E.g., if I download Skype to chat with friends, I have to ensure that those friends also download Skype, register, and add me as a friend so we can chat. Those new users would bring in others.

2. *SEO*: Can the product benefit from SEO and how easy will it be to SEO optimize it?

3. *Busy-Parent Proof*: Does this product require a lot of the parent's time? Or will it still be useful with minimal parental intervention? The less time it requires, the better.

4. *Ease of Adoption*: Does this product require a lot of set up where users have to jump through lots of hoops before it can be used?

5. *Clear Pain Point*: An obvious one: does this product solve a very obvious pain point? A 'yes' is preferable.

6. *Engagement*: How engaging is the product.

7. *Monetizability*: How easy is it to monetize this product using existing models like ads, subscription, etc.?

8. *Low Maintenance*: Does the product need a lot of maintenance? Does the underlying platform update often lead to the product needing regular work to stay compatible (very much an issue in the app)? Low maintenance is always good.

9. *Low 3rd Party Dependency*: E.g., Facebook Apps depend a lot on Facebook's policies, which are constantly changing. It may lead to a rework, or even at times, a total nixing of the product.

10. *Copy Proof*: How easy is it for any random Tom, Dick or Harish to create a copycat?

This is what the analysis looked like:

	Virality	SEO	Busy-Parent Proof	Ease of Adoption	Clear Pain Point	Engagement	Monetizability	Low Maintenance	Low 3rd Party Dependency	Copy Proof	OK Go?
1 Blog (Targeting Parents)		1	1	1		1	1	1	1		✓
2 Curated Contents (YouTube)		1	1	3	1	1					
3 Games (3rd Party Flash)		1	1	3		3	1	1	1	1	✓
4 Games (In-house HTML5)		1	3	1			1	1	1	1	✓
5 Kill My Time (Facebook App)			1	1		1				1	
6 Kill My Time (iOS App)			1	1		1	1	1	3	1	✓
7 Kill My Time (Web App)			1	1		1	1	1	1		
8 Let Teens Be (Facebook App)	1			1	1	1				1	
9 My Public Profile (Facebook App)	1			1	1	1				1	
10 My Sketch Roo (Facebook App)	1		1	1		1				1	
11 My Sketch Roo (iOS App)				3		1	1	1	1	1	
12 My Sketch Roo (Web App)	1	1	1	1		1	1	1	1	1	✓
13 Private Family Media App (Android App)					1				1	1	
14 Private Family Network	1				1				1	1	
15 Roo Kids (iOS App)	1		1	1	1	1		1	1	1	✓
16 Safe Email (Gmail Client)					1	1				1	
17 Safe Social (Facebook Client)					1					1	
18 Sketching Contests (Facebook App)				1		1				1	
19 Sketching Contests (Web App)	1	1	1	1			1	1	1	1	✓
20 Trace My Pix (Facebook App)						1				1	
21 Trace My Pix (Web App)	1	1	1	1		1				1	✓
22 War of Galaxies (Trading Cards)						1		1	3	1	✓
23 Kids App Reviews		1				1	1	1	1	1	✓

Figure 26-3: Prioritizing Between Products

Based on these 10 factors, we narrowed down to a smaller list of products to work on.

We then grouped similar ones and created a more focused set of products to work on.

The rest was purged, deleted, and taken offline. This was not that easy. We had worked a lot on these products, and naturally, we were emotionally attached to them. They were like our babies, and it almost felt like we were harming our own babies. But it had to be done.

7

We now came down to just 7 products. The rest of the year was focused on these seven products:

ContestFu.com – Art, Sketching, Sketching Contests

DigParenting.com (as in we dig parenting) – Articles Targeting Parents and Kids app reviews

Roo Kids – Instant Messaging App

Kill My Time – A quiz app

Gungroo.com – Games for Kids

Warofga – War of Galaxies Trading Cards

My Sketch Roo – Sketching iOS app

Keeping At It (Rest of 2014)

23 products in 2 years by a team of 4 *is* crazy. We had to do it to explore the landscape. Now that we learned what we had learned, we purged a bunch of products to focus on just 7 of them. We worked on all 7 of them for the most part of 2014. The products were:

ContestFu

Figure 26-4: ContestFu Logo

For a Martial Arts movie buff, nothing is more exciting than picking a name that ends in Fu! Hence, ContestFu.

We took all the contests from Gungroo.com and rebranded them as ContestFu.com. We continued to run online contests under the new brand where we gave two prizes: 1/ the most voted, and 2/ the best entry picked by staff.

To vote, one had to Like, Tweet or Register + Up Vote the entry. This ensured growth. The entrants were going around asking people to visit contestfu.com and vote for them.

Initially, we gave an iPod Shuffle as the prize. But as we conducted more contests, we had to bring down the value of the prize.

The product was ready! We just had to monetize it now. A new person joined the team with just one mission: Get schools to use ContestFu to organize art contests. We would charge schools, charge parents, or get a sponsor.

We were quite successful!

Figure 26-5: Drawing Contest in Early Stage School

Small schools were extremely open to the idea. Some schools allowed us to charge INR 50 (around $1.00) per student. Some schools paid for the students and some schools asked us to feel free to get a sponsor.

We even conducted an art contest in a big chain school. They had 108 branches, and around 3,500 students participated in the contest. It was a wonderful time!

Figure 26-6: Entry from a Drawing Contest in Early Stage School

But we had a tough time with well-known schools and international schools. They were our hope for larger revenues. However, things didn't go as expected.

It turns out that all such mega-brand schools have Biz Dev guys. Their job is to help schools get extra revenues. So, whenever we pitched Art Contests to such schools, we used to get asked how much we could pay the school as a fee. Their logic was that the school was giving us access to kids of HNIs (High Networth Individuals) and foreigners. This certainly was of some worth to us as part of our investor pitch.

This dashed our hopes of making money from such schools by organizing contests for them.

Another thing with selling to schools is that each sales cycle is exactly the same as selling to the school before. Typically, once you sell to one client, the subsequent sales cycle is small as you have brand reputation, case studies of benefit to the buyer, etc. But in the case of a school, we had to start from scratch with each new school we approached.

At times, mentioning that another school had used us for the Art contest was actually a detriment.

While we got very encouraging responses from small- and medium-sized schools, we just did not have the bandwidth to target them. The return per school was low, and we needed more feet on the ground to cover more schools. This meant a whole different kind of org than what we wanted to be.

DigParenting

Dig Parenting

Figure 26-7: DigParenting Logo

This was a WordPress-based site built on a commercially available theme. We wanted to keep the dev time minimum and focus all available time on producing content.

We posted 'Top 10' kind of articles a lot. These were very popular and got a lot of traffic from Google and other search engines.

We also wrote reviews of the kids' apps. Initially, we did it for free. But soon, the number of requests overran us. We started charging for reviews with appropriate disclosures. People would pay us via PayPal to write reviews.

We reviewed only those apps that were for kids or parents. This meant that the overall quality of the apps we reviewed was high. We gave an app score between 1-5 based on these three criteria:

Learn, *Fun* and *User Experience*.

We made good money from this. App developers found us, and we did not have to go out hunting for business. We had very good SEO and Google Page Rank and Alexa Page rank. It was a wonderful time!

However, ads and review fees cannot sustain a whole company. The scale of revenue growth was also not there. Also, we were not natural content creators. This meant a whole different kind of org than what we wanted to be.

Gungroo

Figure 26-8: Gungroo Logo

Our flagship website was now a gaming site. We had around 700+ odd games on it. We had games for various categories, for various age groups, for different platforms, sorted by popularity, recently uploaded, last played, etc.

We saw an amazing growth in page views. In fact, the founder of another startup told me that he was talking to his kid sister and she told him that she loved playing kiddie games on a site called Gungroo.com.

He knew me well and was quite excited for me. It was a wonderful time!

But, we had a tough time getting ads for this site on a regular basis. We kept getting rejected even by Google Ads. Kids games get commoditized very fast. Once a game is popular, multiple versions show up. We were not too keen on being game designers either. Just gathering games on our platform to be an SEO magnet wasn't exciting either. This meant a whole different kind of org than what we wanted to be.

Kill My Time

Figure 26-9: Kill My Time iOS App Icon

This iOS app came from a web app and a Facebook app of the same name, and another web app called My GK Fun.

This product did not get purged and made it to the final 7 as it required almost zero-maintenance as an iOS app. There were around 700 or so questions. The UI was good and engagement was high.

It was a paid app. So, it just hung around in the App Store, and once in a while, someone would buy it. It was revenue earned from a one-time investment. Users did download it, and we made some revenue from it.

My Sketch Roo

Figure 26-10: My Sketch Roo iOS App Icon

Our 'kids love sketching' idea now lived in two forms: 1/ ContestFu.com and 2/My Sketch Roo iOS app.

My Sketch Roo had a very simple interface. When other sketching apps on iOS were trying to be super-sophisticated and feature-rich, we chose to be simple. We did not let sophistications or features come in between kids and their sketches.

Figure 26-11: My Sketch Roo Screenshots on iPad

We took the app to the next level by adding coloring books. Kids could download these books and color them. This was both fun and educational. Our English alphabet based coloring books were very popular.

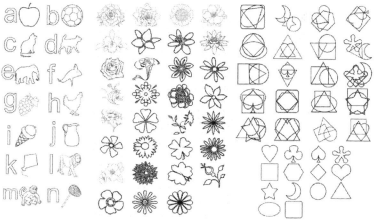

Figure 26-12: My Sketch Roo Coloring Books

We see regular downloads and some of the coloring books are in-app purchase. However, this is just another app. Not something that will take us, as a startup, to another level. Though better positioned than 'Kill My Time', it was still not something we could peg our future on.

Roo Kids

Figure 26-13: Roo Kids Logo

Roo Kids is a safe & fun instant messaging app for kids with minimum yet critical parental controls.

All through our experiments, our original idea that kids need a safe social alternative did not wither away. We kept thinking about it. Out of all the learning, came Roo Kids.

The thing with Facebook and Gmail-like products was that lots of data were retained on our servers. That was a big safety risk. WhatsApp was extremely popular. So, we decided to give Instant Messaging a try. In the case of Instant Message, once a message is delivered, we could just remove it from our servers.

VCs love X for Y analogies. So, we got described as 'Whatsapp for Kids' and at times 'WhatsApp for Kids with Safety'.

We knew parents wanted their kids to explore, learn and master the digital world. But, talking to them, we realized there were 2 very critical concerns the parents had:

- Kids talking to strangers, and
- Kids getting distracted during homework time or sleep time.

We took on these two concerns head-on. The key features of Roo Kids that addressed these concerns were:

- Parents get to review and disapprove anyone in their kid's Contact list. Thus, no stranger or unwanted person could sneak in,
- Kids can block any user or message with immediate effect, and
- Parents can set curfew time slots during which the live chat will not work.

The app was targeted towards kids of ages 6-12 years and was to be used under parental supervision. We built iPhone, iPad, Android and Kindle versions.

We believe that it is good for kids to experience a restricted app such as Roo Kids before moving into social networking sites, which provides less safety.

Finally, we had a product-market fit that we wanted to keep working on and could bet our future on!

War of Fascinating Galaxies

Figure 26-14: War of Galaxies Artwork

If a kid knows about Princess Apsa, Prince Kowal, the Sombrero Galaxy or the Hoag's Object, they have definitely played with the WarOFGa Trading cards.

Figure 26-15: War of Galaxies Trading Cards

We started with 2 sets of 19 cards each for INR 50 (around $1.00). One had a pink back and the other had a blue back. One of those 'for boys' and 'for girls' things. The content was all same — the color was the only different feature. Interestingly, the pink sets sold more across genders.

Figure 26-16: War of Galaxies Trading Cards Sets

We then sold packs of 32 cards for $1.50 (INR 75). These continued to sell very well at city fairs and other places. It was a wonderful time!

But like before, we just could not get them to sell online. We did not want to develop distribution channels like other offline products either. This meant a whole different kind of org than what we wanted to be.

So, all through 2014, we did well with most of our 7 products and were making small revenues from them. We had also learned a bunch of new lessons in 2014. It turned out that we were still stretched thin. It was time to rethink what we should focus on. Maybe another purge?

· · ·

The Second Purge (Early 2015)

7 products. Each a whole startup in itself. Small team. Limited resources.

This meant only one thing: Go all in on one of these, drop the rest, and not get distracted by any more spin-off & *focus*.

Finding Our Sunday Passion

So, which product should we choose from the 7? One we would love to work on even on a Sunday and whose growth will give us a reason to celebrate on weekends.

We went back to the earlier method I had described earlier.

The Analysis

We dropped the criteria for which all 7 were doing well. We chose the following 7 factors to score each product on. The one with a maximum score would win!

1. *Virality*: We defined virality as growth driven by a user where they had to bring other users to the product or the platform for it to be of use. E.g., if I download Skype to chat with friends, I have to ensure that those friends also download Skype, register and add me as a friend so we can chat. Those new users would bring in others.

2. *SEO*: Can the product benefit from SEO and how easy will it be to search-engine optimize it?

3. *Clear Pain Point*: An obvious one: does this product solve a very obvious pain point? A 'yes' is preferable.

4. *Monetizability*: How easy is it to monetize this product using existing models like ads, subscription, etc.

5. *Uniqueness*: Do we stand out among other offerings in the Kid's app market? While first-mover advantage was not something we sought, some degree of uniqueness was preferred.

6. *Global Market*: We wanted to reach out to global markets. As we are based in India, it is a market of interest for us. Indians prefer to be on Global platforms. A quick look at top apps in any B2C (non-ecommerce) category quickly confirms this. So, if we did well globally, we would automatically do well in India.

7. *No User-Customer Conflict*: I have talked about User-Customer conflict earlier. This conflict is very evident in Kids' products. The users are the kids, and the customers are the parents. It is a tightrope to walk while balancing interests and ROI for both.

Below is the result of the analysis:

		About	Virality	SEO	Clear Pain Point	Monetizability	Uniqueness	Global Market	No User-Customer Conflict	OK Go?
1	ContestFU	Platform for Art Contests	1	1		1			1	
2	Dig Parenting	Content for Parents		1				1	1	
3	Gungroo	Games		1				1	1	
4	Kill My Time	iOS based Quiz App						1	1	
5	My Sketch Roo	iOS based Sketching App				1		1	1	
6	Roo Kids	"Whatsapp for Kids"	1		1	1	1	1		✓
7	Fascinating Galaxies	Trading Cards				1	1		1	

Figure 26-17: Prioritizing Between Products

So, Roo Kids it was!

• • •

Roo Kids

The first thing we had to decide was which device to target first. We had learned the lesson to not go all out till we get sufficient feedback from the market.

Our studies showed that while Phones were personal devices, the iPad gets passed around in the home most. It was replacing the Home PC as the default family device. So, we targeted it first.

Figure 26-18: Roo Kids Product Roadmap

Once the iPad version was out, we were able to reuse the code to add an iPhone layout and release an iPhone/iPod version.

The Android version took some time to start. We were seeing enough traction, usage, and feedback from iOS versions. But as soon as things stabilized, we released an Android version.

We got a lot of requests to add Kindle Fire support. Many parents had bought it, and the device had a strong reputation for being child-safe. With some changes (In-app purchase, notification, gathering device token, etc.), we reused the Android code and released the Kindle version.

How's Roo Kids Doing?

The app has been out for enough time for us to know if our analysis was right. Is it what the analysis had promised it could be? Let's see:

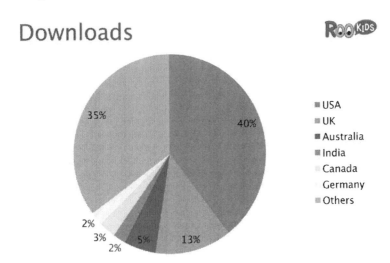

Figure 26-19: Roo Kids Download Stats

This includes messages sent to other users, messages sent to canned-response chatbots like Echo, Puzzle, Science for Ages 8/9, stickers, images, and doodles.

Messages

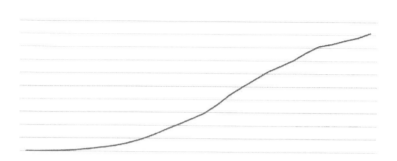

Figure 26-20: Roo Kids Messages Stats

Stat commonly used to measure active users on Social Networks and Messaging apps. The number of unique users who have used the app at least once in a month.

These statistics look very encouraging. The analysis was right and it was a good call to go all-in on Roo Kids.

Encouraged by user response, we are now expanding Roo Kids products to include some cool features and become a default safe social for kids.

We are also fundraising and we welcome all interests or queries from investors.

In the next chapter, I discuss lessons learned that other startups (in general) and startups for kids (in particular) may find useful.

A version of this appeared on www.ddiinnxx.com.

27.
Lessons From a Failing Startup

I always start by pointing out, it is failing and not failed! No one has given up. The journey is still on.

But, why failing? I believe that a startup is failing and dying every day. The day that stops, you have become a regular business. Even if you are profitable, you are still failing as you should be taking leaps and risks that can bring you down to the ground. This is how I define a startup.

To conclude the series, it makes sense to share my take on startups and lessons learned. So here we go:

1. Co-Founders

If you can't find a right co-founder, go solo! Do not get a co-founder because everyone says so.

I decided to go solo. Hence, I am in a good position to give advice on co-founders! You know, at times, the bystander has more clue than the people in the middle of a mess.

a. Be Prepared For Failure

Discuss failure and imminent closure. Discuss how you will disband the startup.

b. Be Prepared For Success

Nothing impedes like success. When that first big deal comes in. When that large chunk of cash comes in. When the pictures show up in the newspapers. When that panel guest invitation comes in. Be prepared for that. Who will do what and how will you share the limelight.

Definitely, be clear on how to use that chunk of investor cash.

I know you will have a good plan that you must have discussed with investors against which they invested in you. But plans seldom survive contact with reality. So, discuss how changes in plans will be handled.

c. Be Prepared for Uneventfulness

OK, I don't even know if that is a real word. Still …

90% of your days will be uneventful. You will do what you were doing the day before. Many days, you will have no clue what to do next.

This is the biggest secret ever kept. Not all days are full of action and results and decisions and power meeting and OK-GO music running as the soundtrack to your life.

Most days are spent doing the same stuff and at times being adrift and clueless on how to make the next big thing happen. You will sit on your desk with your head in your hands, pulling your hair and wondering what you should do to get things to work!

Be ready to see each other in this pose and be seen in this pose.

2. Fund Raising

Unless you have reverse engineered the funding patterns and built a startup that has all the elements investors are looking for, funding is going to be a nightmare.

This is what I mean by reverse engineering the Series A funding patterns: If you are in India, as per current gossip, pick a product that is doing good in the US, be a young male, gather few IIT grads, and go pitch! Or, pick an ecommerce idea, show how you can get millions of rupees to flow through your system (even if 80% of that will come from investors via Discounted Cash Flow), be a young male, gather a few IIT grads, and go pitch!

But I digress.

a. Always Have Investors

Fine, you can bootstrap. Fine, you can generate revenue. Fine, you can do it with your own money. Still!

Nothing challenges your optimism than to sit in front of someone and get him or her to see your vision. You are the entrepreneur. You are the ones with dreams, energy, and will to dent the universe. But if you can't convince even one person to buy in, something is not right.

You need to get an investor to make sure you know that you are a seer and not delusional.

b. Find an Entrepreneur-Investor

All my early investors were entrepreneurs themselves. They had seen failures and tough days and have achieved big success.

Every once in a while, I get an, "I hear you! Keep going. It's a marathon, not a sprint."

Nothing strengthens your core than someone who has followed the *pagdandi* (the beaten path) and found success.

Also, there is one more thing: It has to be their own money they are investing. They will decide to invest in you based on the same gut feeling and analytics that made them successful in the first place. This is a massive upvote!

c. Say No to Institutional Money

Here is how I think VCs work. They take a bunch of money from rich people and organizations and promise them some x returns in no time. Say 10x return in 7 years. Along the way, they assure them that their money will make the lives of poor, middle class, diseased, etc., better.

The only (and big) difference between someone who is investing his or her own money and another who is investing someone else's money is the flexibility on time!

Never hesitate to take money from an entrepreneur. Think a lot before taking it from a VC, especially during your early days. Go to a VC when you are sure you can get them the returns on their investment in a predictable span of time.

3. Conserve Cash

Cash in hand is the only friend you have. Conserve it. Instead of paying someone in cash, see if you can pay back in kind. Pay closer to due dates. Don't spend on something you did not need critically yesterday or last week. Try trial versions before buying the full product. Use open source or free versions.

4. Get a Life

If your startup is the only thing going for you, here is what you need to do: get a life!

Very soon, you will run out of money or ideas or friends or energy or all of these in one go. What will you turn to then? How will you get your groove back?

Nothing invigorates me like a short trip to a nature-rich destination. You should find something similar.

5. Pivot, Experiment, Concede, Change

Very rarely does a successful startup get everything right from the very beginning. So, be ready to pivot around one successful aspect of your startup, experiment, concede when you are wrong, and change.

Success is directly proportional to your elasticity and plasticity.

6. Lead from the Front

Be a leader of your team. They will turn to you for vision, direction, ideas, etc. Always be a few steps ahead of them. This means that you have to work harder than anyone else in the team.

Always be full of ideas for them to try out. Always be ready to focus on what's next, rather than failure. Don't waste time blaming them and spend time nudging them into new directions.

7. Hiring & Firing

Hire people that are better and smarter than you. Give them a purpose and direction, be transparent about how they will be judged, and then get out of their way!

Also, if you hire a person who is not right for the task, fire early. No point letting them continue. They will not have a good time working with you, others working with them will not have a good time, and you will be burning cash!

Guide them in finding a job that suits them best and let go.

Do not turn a misfit employee into your favorite project. Do not believe you can make it work somehow, however smart or great a people person you are.

Other hardworking and performing employees will feel demotivated when they see an under-performer getting the same benefits. The under-performer will feel bad that in spite of being smart and hardworking, your startup is unable to give the role he or she can excel in.

It is not going to work, and all involved will suffer.

8. Personality

Forget aura, charisma, reality-distortion field, etc. Develop a sense of humor (the self-deprecating kind is best), learn to praise others and be patient (not dragging or delaying) when dealing with people.

Conclusion

In conclusion to this series: It has been a wonderful journey, I met a lot of wonderful people, and I learned a lot about myself.

My aim is to treat kids more than just a school-going, IQ-improving, and exam-passing bots. They are individuals who have a purpose and personality of their own and deserve the best of new technology and innovations. Roo Kid is one of the ways I am working on this aim.

I hope to succeed in building a neat product and taking it to the right audience. Along the way, I will have fun, meet more wonderful people, make a difference in lives, and maybe make money!

Wish me luck!

A version of this appeared on www.ddiinnxx.com.

About The Author

Dinker Charak is interdisciplinary who writes fiction, science fiction, and about entrepreneurship and Product Management.

During his career, he has built software products that have been part of Real-time Operating Systems, Paperless Offices, and Home Automation; and that has helped develop Online Video Ads business and founded a startup. Dinker has worked at Fermilab (US) and contributed to CERN (Switzerland), two top research labs that conduct basic research into particle physics. He holds a patent in Advertising Technology.

As personal interests go, Dinker holds Product Management Workshops for startups in collaboration with the Indian Institute of Management, Ahmedabad's CIIE, National Association of Software and Services Companies' (NASSCOM) 10,000 Startups, and ThoughtWorks.

He has also authored two collections of short-stories and sci-fi: The Murmurs of the Dawn and Absolute and None, both of which are available on Kindle.

He is ddiinnxx on twitter. If you find a ddiinnxx elsewhere, it is most probably him. You can read his blog on *www.ddiinnxx.com*.

Dinker completed his Master's in Computer Application from the International Institute of Professional Studies, Devi Ahilya University, Indore, India.

Appendix

LIST OF FIGURES

Figure 1-1: Product in A Box Template 5
Figure 1-2: Product in A Box Reference 6
Figure 1-3: Elevator Pitch Template (*http://bit.ly/2GapjJ7*) 7
Figure 1-4: Business Model Canvas (*http://bit.ly/2nXqaX6*) 8
Figure 1-5: Product Stack Template (*http://bit.ly/2Eni4Nu*) 10
Figure 1-6: Product Management Canvas (*http://bit.ly/2qncrvO*) 11
Figure 2-1: Product Backlog in Product Development Process (*http://bit.ly/2EnrHfe*) 25
Figure 3-1: Product Management Canvas (*http://bit.ly/2Hepcxp*) 27
Figure 3-2: Product Management Canvas in Product Development Process (*http://bit.ly/2GbAlOm*) 28
Figure 3-3: Suggested Flow for Filling Up The Product Management Canvas (*http://bit.ly/2CgABsV*) 30
Figure 4-1: Competition Analysis – Us and Them (*http://bit.ly/2nXJx2j*) .. 36
Figure 4-2: The Four Boxes of Competition Analysis (*http://bit.ly/2CkmByj*) 37
Figure 4-3: Competition Analysis Template (*http://bit.ly/2CkmNO3*) 38
Figure 5-1: Golden Logarithmic Spiral (*http://bit.ly/2Ep8A4l*) 41
Figure 5-2: Internal to External - The Golden Curve (*http://bit.ly/2Gay45Y*) 42
Figure 5-3: Internal to External - Stage 1 (*http://bit.ly/2Ep9i1J*) 42
Figure 5-4: Internal to External - Stage 2 (*http://bit.ly/2Ganf3S*) 43
Figure 5-5: Internal to External - Stage 3 (*http://bit.ly/2Gcsgsy*) 43
Figure 5-6: Internal to External - Stage 4 (*http://bit.ly/2nXoc8Z*) 44
Figure 5-7: Internal to External - Stage 5 (*http://bit.ly/2F2nij5*) 44
Figure 5-8: Internal to External - Stage 6 (*http://bit.ly/2nXfK9F*) 45
Figure 5-9: Internal to External – Tasks at Various Stages (*http://bit.ly/2Er5zjS*) 46

Figure 6-1: Sample Pricing Table (*http://bit.ly/2nZ3cia*) 52

Figure 8-1: The Three-Circles of Product Thinking (*http://bit.ly/2ClYZK0*) 59

Figure 11-1: Five Buckets of Product Management (*http://bit.ly/2Ekr45Z*) 65

Figure 11-2: Five Buckets of Product Management for Ideator/Disruptor/Startup ProMa (*http://bit.ly/2EpFGBn*) 68

Figure 11-3: Five Buckets of Product Management for Incremental Innovator/Enterprise ProMa (*http://bit.ly/2EY5lBX*) 69

Figure 11-4: Five Buckets of Product Management for Sustenance Stage Product ProMa (*http://bit.ly/2Cktuje*) 70

Figure 11-5: Five Buckets of Product Management for Domain-Specific Product ProMa (*http://bit.ly/2GbxYv7*) 71

Figure 16-1: Scientific Process by Francis Bacon (*http://bit.ly/2GaYWD4*). 80

Figure 16-2: Build-Measure-Learn by Francis Bacon (*http://bit.ly/2nZQXSs*) 81

Figure 16-3: Scientific Process by René Descartes (*http://bit.ly/2GaCgTd*) . 82

Figure 16-4: Build-Measure-Learn (*http://bit.ly/2CixeC0*) 82

Figure 16-5: ArchonMagnus' Modern Scientific Process (*http://bit.ly/2F2KfTb*) 83

Figure 16-6: Modern Scientific Process as Product Development Process (*http://bit.ly/2GaCgmb*) 85

Figure 17-1: Actors in Modern Product Development Process (*http://bit.ly/2GaCfP9*) 87

Figure 19-1: MVP of a Data Platform (*http://bit.ly/2EM9yqQ*) 91

Figure 20-1: Awareness of Consequences vis-à-vis Degrees of Separation (*http://bit.ly/2Cjtno0*) 95

Figure 23-1: MVP from Lean Enterprise by Jez Humble, Joanne Molesky and Barry O'Reilly 100

Figure 23-2: Maslow's Hierarchy of Needs (*http://bit.ly/2Cj2K2H*) 101

Figure 23-3: Startups and Maslow's Hierarchy (*http://bit.ly/2CjZvrH*) 102

Figure 26-1: Two Password Login (*http://bit.ly/2Ekr4D1*) 110

Figure 26-2: Safe Web Solutions from Gungroo Highlighted on Home Page (*http://bit.ly/2Emsddf*) 112

Figure 26-3: Prioritizing Between Products (*http://bit.ly/2HedYt8*) 121

Figure 26-4: ContestFu Logo (*http://bit.ly/2Eo47iy*) 122

Figure 26-5: Drawing Contest in Early Stage School (*http://bit.ly/2G8gKi7*) 123

Figure 26-6: Entry from a Drawing Contest in Early Stage School (*http://bit.ly/2Cixgd6*) 124

Figure 26-7: DigParenting Logo (*http://bit.ly/2HedZxc*) 125

Figure 26-8: Gungroo Logo (*http://bit.ly/2Enf7fL*) 126

Figure 26-9: Kill My Time iOS App Icon (*http://bit.ly/2F1sXpf*) 127

Figure 26-10: My Sketch Roo iOS App Icon (*http://bit.ly/2CiFfGT*) 128

Figure 26-11: My Sketch Roo Screenshots on iPad (*http://bit.ly/2EnkLi4*) 129

Figure 26-12: My Sketch Roo Coloring Books (*http://bit.ly/2GaYXa6*) ... 129

Figure 26-13: Roo Kids Logo (*http://bit.ly/2HcIiE9*) 130

Figure 26-14: War of Galaxies Artwork (*http://bit.ly/2o2xUHt*) 131

Figure 26-15: War of Galaxies Trading Cards (*http://bit.ly/2HedXW6*) ... 132

Figure 26-16: War of Galaxies Trading Cards Sets (*http://bit.ly/2Hfm84q*) 132

Figure 26-17: Prioritizing Between Products (*http://bit.ly/2GaCiuj*) 135

Figure 26-18: Roo Kids Product Roadmap (*http://bit.ly/2GaChqf*) 135

Figure 26-19: Roo Kids Download Stats (*http://bit.ly/2CiGCWh*) 136

Figure 26-20: Roo Kids Messages Stats (*http://bit.ly/2EozHg5*) 137

List of Tables

Table 1-1: Hackathon Agenda 3
Table 1-2: Suggested Paper Size for Various Artifacts 12
Table 2-1: Product Backlog Card Template 16
Table 2-2: Template for Scoping Feature 18
Table 2-3: Template for Scoping Feature 21
Table 2-4: Example for Scoping Feature A 23
Table 2-5: Example for Scoping Feature B 24
Table 5-1: Internal vs External 39
Table 14-1: Product Manager's RACI 76
Table 14-2: Product Entrepreneur's RACI 77

VIDEOS & DECKS

Videos (YouTube)

A talk on Su-Ha-Ri (*http://bit.ly/2BTVgHO*)

Product Management in the Context of Consulting (*http://bit.ly/2nT2hjs*)

The Edge of Product Management (*http://bit.ly/2G4XiTg*)

Panel Discussion on Moving into Product Management (*http://bit.ly/2o5HZCG*)

Panel Discussion on How to decide what to build next (*http://bit.ly/2BU3KyD*)

Decks (SlideShare)

Using Product Management Canvas (*http://bit.ly/2nWx8LQ*)

Taking In-House Product to Market (*http://bit.ly/2nXZrsu*)

Shuhari: Learn - Digress - Transcend (*http://bit.ly/2svnGE4*)

Five Buckets Model for Product Management (*http://bit.ly/2ElPkVw*)

Product Management in the Context of Consulting (*http://bit.ly/2o0zl8n*)

The Edge of Product Management (*http://bit.ly/2Emj4pr*)

Building products - It takes a village (*http://bit.ly/2EXZXPm*)

7 Reasons Why Your Product Will Fail (*http://bit.ly/2nVjxEB*)

Reference

Hackathon: From Idea to a Product in a Day

[1] Tweet. CIIE, IIM Ahmedabad. Accessed January 2018. <https://twitter.com/ciieindia/status/695588967731703808>

[2] Post. NASSCOM 10,000 Startups. Accessed January 2018. <https://www.facebook.com/events/1711978709098857/>

[3] Idea to Product – A Product Management Workshop. Dinker Charak. Accessed January 2018. <http://10000startups.com/idea-to-product-a-product-management-workshop/>

[4] Inception workshop - Kickstarting an Agile project in style. Jenny Wong. Accessed January 2018. <https://www.slideshare.net/JennyWong8/inception-workshop-kickstarting-an-agile-workshop-30772352>

[5] Product in a Box. Luke Hohmann. Accessed January 2018. Innovation Games: Creating Breakthrough Products Through Collaborative Play 1st Edition

[6] The Agile Warrior. Jonathan Rasmussin. Accessed January 2018. <https://agilewarrior.wordpress.com/2010/11/06/the-agile-inception-deck/>

[7] Business Model Generation. Alexander Osterwalder, Yves Pigneur. Accessed January 2018. <https://strategyzer.com/> Sharable under Creative Commons Attribution-ShareAlike 3.0 Unported (CC BY-SA 3.0)

[8] User intent analysis engine. Diaz Nesamoney, Parth S. Chandra, Dinker Charak, Sanjay Dahiya, Sandeep Kumar, Hans Guntren. Accessed January 2018. <https://www.google.com/patents/US20120136714>

[9] Sharable under Creative Commons (CC BY-SA 3.0). Dinker Charak. <http://www.ddiinnxx.com/hackathon-idea-product-day/>

[10] Sharable under Creative Commons (CC BY-SA 3.0). Dinker Charak. <http://www.ddiinnxx.com/hackathon-idea-product-day/>

Product Backlog

[1] What is a Backlog? Agile Alliance. Accessed January 2018. <https://www.agilealliance.org/glossary/backlog/>

² Scrum Product Backlog? Mountain Goat Software. Accessed January 2018. <https://www.mountaingoatsoftware.com/agile/scrum/product-backlog>

³ The product backlog: your ultimate to-do list. Dan Radigan. Accessed January 2018. <https://www.atlassian.com/agile/scrum/backlogs>

⁴ Inception workshop - Kickstarting an Agile project in style. Jenny Wong. Accessed January 2018. <https://www.slideshare.net/JennyWong8/inception-workshop-kickstarting-an-agile-workshop-30772352>

Product Management Canvas – Product in a Snapshot

¹ THE PRODUCT CANVAS. Roman Pichler. Accessed January 2018. <https://www.romanpichler.com/blog/the-product-canvas/>

² Working with Epics. Atlassian Support. Accessed January 2018. <https://confluence.atlassian.com/agile/jira-agile-user-s-guide/working-with-epics>

³ User Story. Wikipedia. Accessed January 2018. <https://en.wikipedia.org/wiki/User_story>

⁴ Monthly active users. Wikipedia. Accessed January 2018. <https://en.wikipedia.org/wiki/Monthly_active_users>

⁵ Product Evangelism. Marty Cagan. Accessed January 2018. <https://svpg.com/product-evangelism/>

⁶ SSL Certificate Renewal: Even Google Forgets. SSL Shopper. Accessed January 2018. <https://www.sslshopper.com/article-ssl-certificate-renewal-even-google-forgets.html>

⁷ Oops: Instagram forgot to renew its SSL certificate. Owen Williams. Accessed January 2018. <https://thenextweb.com/apps/2015/04/30/oops-instagram-forgot-to-renew-its-ssl-certificate/>

⁸ Apple neglects to renew SSL certificate, breaks Software Update in the process. Nick Mediati. Accessed January 2018. <https://www.macworld.com/article/2158788/apple-neglects-to-renew-ssl-certificate-breaks-software-update-in-the-process.html>

Competition Analysis in 3 Simple Steps

¹ Competitive Analysis for Startups: The Goal. Raymond. Accessed January 2018. <http://www.flowventures.com/competitive-analysis-for-startups-the-goal/>

Taking In-House Product To Market

[1] Managing Internal vs. External Products. Proficientz.com. Accessed January 2018. <https://www.proficientz.com/project-portfolio-vs-product-portfolio/>

Product Thinking = UX Design + Project Management + Business Model

[1] End product. Dictionary.com. Accessed January 2018. <http://www.dictionary.com/browse/end-product>

[2] Why Product Thinking is the next big thing in UX Design. Nikkel Blaase. Accessed January 2018. <https://medium.com/@jaf_designer/why-product-thinking-is-the-next-big-thing-in-ux-design-ee7de959f3fe>

Shuhari: Learn – Digress – Transcend

[1] ShuHaRi Japanese Learning System. Arno Koch. Accessed January 2018. <http://www.makigami.info/shuhari-japanese-learning-system/>

[2] Livedoor Blog. BizPos. Accessed January 2018. <http://blog.livedoor.jp/bizpos/archives/51316464.html>

[3] ShuHaRi. Martin Fowler. Accessed January 2018. <https://martinfowler.com/bliki/ShuHaRi.html>

Five Buckets Model for Product Management

[1] The Five Competencies of User Experience Design. Steve Psomas. Accessed January 2018. <https://www.uxmatters.com/mt/archives/2007/11/the-five-competencies-of-user-experience-design.php>

[2] Cultural impact of Star Wars. Wikipedia. Accessed January 2018. <https://en.wikipedia.org/wiki/The_Force_(Star_Wars)#Cultural_impact>

[3] Reality distortion field. Wikipedia. Accessed February 2018. <https://en.wikipedia.org/wiki/Reality_distortion_field>

The Product Sociologist

[1] Sociology. Wikipedia. Accessed January 2018. <https://en.wikipedia.org/wiki/Sociology>

[2] What is Sociology? Department of Sociology, The University of North Carolina at Chapel Hill. Accessed January 2018. <https://sociology.unc.edu/undergraduate-program/sociology-major/what-is-sociology/>

[3] Category: Sociology. Wikipedia. Accessed January 2018.
<https://en.wikipedia.org/wiki/Category:Sociology>

[4] 'No Man is an Island'. Geoff Johnston's Blog. Accessed February 2018.
<https://web.cs.dal.ca/~johnston/poetry/island.html>

[5] John Donne. Wikipedia. Accessed February 2018.
<https://en.wikipedia.org/wiki/John_Donne>

[6] Robot series (Asimov). Wikipedia. Accessed February 2018.
<https://en.wikipedia.org/wiki/Robot_series_(Asimov)>

Waterfall vs Agile: An Age-Old Battle

[1] Charvaka. Wikipedia. Accessed January 2018.
<https://en.wikipedia.org/wiki/Charvaka>

Product Development & Scientific Process

[1] Bacon's view of induction. Wikipedia. Accessed January 2018.
<https://en.wikipedia.org/wiki/Baconian_method#Bacon's_view_of_induction>

[2] The Scientific Method as an Ongoing Process. ArchonMagnus. Accessed January 2018.
<https://commons.wikimedia.org/w/index.php?curid=42164616>

[3] Five Whys Technique. Asian Development Bank. Accessed February 2018.
<http://www.adb.org/publications/five-whys-technique>

[4] The 4W1H method for understanding Customer Needs! Gowtham Injamuri. Accessed February 2018.
<https://medium.com/@gowthaminjamuri/the-4w1h-method-for-understanding-customer-needs-b64cf6a47afb>

[5] Measuring the User Experience on a Large Scale: User-Centered Metrics for Web Applications. Kerry Rodden, Hilary Hutchinson, Xin Fu. Accessed February 2018. <https://research.google.com/pubs/pub36299.html>

[6] Crouch; Sunny Crouch; Matthew Housden (2003). Marketing research for managers; The Marketing Series; Chartered Institute of Marketing. Butterworth-Heinemann. p. 22. ISBN 0750654538.

7 Reasons Why Your Product Will Fail

[1] Five Dangerous Lessons to Learn From Steve Jobs. Chunka Mui. Accessed January 2018. <https://www.forbes.com/sites/chunkamui/2011/10/17/five-dangerous-lessons-to-learn-from-steve-jobs/>

[2] The MAYA Principle: Design for the Future, but Balance it with Your Users' Present. Rikke Dam. Accessed January 2018. <https://www.interaction-design.org/literature/article/design-for-the-future-but-balance-it-with-your-users-present>

[3] Apple "Switch" Ad Campaign. applefandan. Accessed January 2018. <https://www.youtube.com/watch?v=VHid1bcf1sM>

[4] "I'm a Mac I'm a PC". MacTechHowTo. Accessed January 2018. <https://www.youtube.com/watch?v=qfv6Ah_MVJU>

[5] What Is a Business Model? Andrea Ovans. Accessed January 2018. <https://hbr.org/2015/01/what-is-a-business-model>

[6] How Do You "Design" Trust Between Strangers? Guy Raz, Host. Accessed January 2018. <https://www.npr.org/templates/transcript/transcript.php?storyId=478563991>

MVP of a Data Platform

[1] StranglerApplication. Martin Fowler, Host. Accessed April 2018. <https://www.martinfowler.com/bliki/StranglerApplication.html>

Are Startups an MVP for Maslow's Hierarchy?

[1] 'Figure 4-5: Minimum Viable Product: build a slice across instead of one layer at a time' [image], in Jez Humble, Joanne Molesky, Barry O'Reilly 2015, Lean Enterprise, O'Reilly, India, Second Indian Reprint, p. 77. This diagram was inspired by Jussi Pasanen, with acknowledgment to Aarron Walter, Ben Tollady, Ben Rowe, Lexi Thorn, and Senthil Kugalur.

[2] Maslow's hierarchy of needs. Wikipedia. Accessed January 2018. <https://en.wikipedia.org/wiki/Maslow%27s_hierarchy_of_needs>

Our Children and The Digital Future – A Manifesto

[1] Manifesto for Agile Software Development. Various Signatories. Accessed January 2018. <http://agilemanifesto.org/>

Failing Since 2012

[1] Helicopter Parenting. Healthy Living Magazine. Weber, Jill. Accessed February 2018. <http://www.healthylivingmagazine.us/Articles/641/>

[2] Gungroo - WarOFGa - Trading Cards One on One. Gungroo Software. Accessed February 2018. <https://www.youtube.com/watch?v=7on6DtTknLc>

[3] Gungroo - WarOFGa - Trading Cards Memorizing. Gungroo Software. Accessed February 2018. *<https://www.youtube.com/watch?v=NapRUyI4A1I>*

[4] War of Galaxies – A Sci-Fi from the Creators of Roo Kids. Gungroo Software. Accessed February 2018. *<http://www.rookidsapp.com/blog/warofgaa/>*

Made in the
USA
Middletown, DE